Please return/renew this item by the last date
above. You can renew on-line at
www.lbhf.gov.uk/libraries
or by phone
0303 123 0035

putting residents first

Hammersmith & Fulham Libraries

Dennis Turner

FULHAM'S
Promotion Seasons

Dennis Turner

First published in Great Britain in 2012 by The Derby Books Publishing Company Limited, 3 The Parker Centre, Derby, DE21 4SZ.

ISBN 9781780910208

Printed and bound by Gomer Press, Llandysul Ceredigion.

Contents

Fulham's Promotion Seasons

1.

The First Silverware: 1931-32

Background

In 1928, Fulham's unbroken membership of the (old) Second Division, which stretched back to 1907 when they were first elected to the Football League, came to a humiliating end. They were relegated to the Third Division South, largely because they contrived to lose 20 of their 21 games away from the Cottage. At home, only divisional champions Manchester City had a better record and centre-forward Sid Elliott actually set a new club scoring record with 26 goals. But on the road, all they had to show for their travels was two points from a possible 42, this after a 1-0 win at Notts County.

The board gave manager Joe Bradshaw a season to get the club back. When the Cottagers could only finish fifth in 1928-29, he departed, to be replaced by Edward (Ned) Liddell, a well-known football personality who included spells with Sunderland, Southampton, Orient, Arsenal and Southend on his CV. He was QPR manager from 1920-24, and then joined Fulham as a scout. Sadly he was no more successful than Bradshaw, and over Easter 1931, when Fulham were destined to finish ninth following the seventh place in his first season (1929-30), Liddell stepped aside and went back to scouting.

The Championship team. Back row, left to right: Oliver, Gibbon, Iceton, Birch, Penn. Front row: Richards, Hammond, Newton, Price, Finch, Gibbons.

In his place came the experienced and outspoken James McIntyre, a man un-encumbered by self-doubt, who looked to Arsenal's legendary manager, Herbert Chapman, as his role model. Born in Walsall in 1881, McIntyre was a journeyman player, initially in non-League football in the Midlands and then spells with Notts County, Northampton, Reading and Coventry between 1902 and 1906. It was in 1907 that he started on the managerial path, as assistant trainer and then trainer at Coventry. In 1912 he went to Southampton in the same capacity but returned to Coventry to work in a munitions factory in the Great War. When football was resumed, he was appointed manager at the Dell and guided Saints to the Third Division South title in 1922. But, two years later, McIntyre left football to run a hotel in Scotland until his old club Coventry lured him back in June 1928 to be their manager. It was from Highfield Road that Fulham recruited him in April 1931.

In the programme editorial for the opening game of the season, the Fulham directors claimed that 'we approach the campaign starting today with more enthusiastic belief in ourselves. The changes in the executive of the club last April were only made after careful thought and consideration, and we are of the opinion that the policy will be justified. We are more determined than ever that every possible effort shall be concentrated on promotion this season.'

Similar sentiments are expressed by most boards in most club programmes at the beginning of most seasons, but in this case these hopes were fulfilled. Fulham won their first piece of domestic silverware, which they had to do to reclaim their Second Division status because only one club was promoted in those days.

Close Season Transfer Activity

Having watched the closing games of 1930-31, McIntyre knew the team needed strengthening. He raised some funds by selling outside-right Jimmy Temple to First Division Sunderland and centre-forward Bill Haley to QPR. To replace them, he went back to his old club Coventry for winger Billy Richards and to Stockport for Frank 'Bonzo' Newton. Both were shrewd signings. Richards was to become the first Fulham player to be capped by Wales while Newton went on to be become a goalscoring phenomenon and a Cottage folk hero. Bonzo was 28 when he signed for just £575. Lancashire-born, he was one of 19 children and had served in the army in India and the Calcutta police before joining Stockport in 1928, where he scored 93 goals in 101 games.

The team which kicked off the season, nevertheless had a familiar look to it. The heart of the side was the impressive half-back line of skipper Len Oliver, Syd 'Carnera' Gibbons and Bert Barrett, who between them played over 1,150 games for Fulham. In goal was old favourite, the fearless Ernie Beecham, with Sonny Gibbon and Bill Hickie at full-backs. These were the positions that caused McIntyre most headaches during the season and he was not slow to make changes. Upfront, he was fortunate to have inherited two very good inside-forwards to play alongside Newton, the clever, scheming Johnny Price and the free-scoring Jim Hammond, fresh from his summer duties as a Sussex county cricketer. On the left wing he started with the long-serving Frank Penn who quickly made way for young Jack Finch. Of this squad, only Beecham, Oliver, Barrett and Penn were in the team that had been relegated in 1928.

Manager James McIntyre.

Bonzo Newton goes head-to-head with Coventry 'keeper Tommy Allen on the opening day of the 1931-32 season.

A Flying Start

The manager, unlike his predecessors, was adept at using the press to attract publicity and his pre-season briefings with journalists raised the supporters' expectations. A sizeable crowd of 17,224 turned up for the opening game, coincidentally against McIntyre's former club, Coventry, and they had a foretaste of what was in store over the coming nine months. Fulham ran out 5-3 winners, with the dynamic duo of Newton (on his debut) and Hammond both scoring twice. The fifth was a Barrett penalty, awarded by referee Stanley Rous (later Sir Stanley) for handball. The two teams drew the return 5-5 at Highfield Road in January and the 18 goals scored in 180 minutes was then a Fulham record aggregate for two games against the same club in a season.

The Cottagers went into the next two games, away at Exeter and at Gillingham, without injured skipper Oliver, for whom Harold Webb deputised. In the west country, Newton got the first of his four hat-tricks that season (he also had another effort disallowed for handball) as Fulham came away with an impressive 3-0 win.

But in Kent, they came a cropper. On a bumpy Priestfield pitch, and in a high wind, the team gave a below par performance and were beaten 2-1. Newton was marked out of the game and only Beecham lived up to his reputation.

It proved only to be temporary setback, however, for on the first Monday in September, Fulham got back to winning ways, and in record-breaking fashion. McIntyre's men scored 10 goals against a weak Torquay side, the club's best-ever League score and their highest since 12 were put past Wellingborough in the Southern League in 1905. Hammond led the way with four goals, ably supported by Newton and Price with two each. Finch, playing his first game of the season in place of Penn, and Joe Proud, replacing the injured Richards, completed the scoring. In reply, Torquay could only manage two, through Hutchinson when the score was 7-0 and Stabb at 8-1.

This emphatic win was the first in a sequence of four straight victories which, by the time Northampton visited the Cottage for the last game in September, left Fulham sharing top spot with Southend and Bournemouth on 12 points. Luton were beaten 3-2 at home days after the Torquay win and then maximum points were taken from visits to Plainmoor and Ninian Park. The return with Torquay was a much closer affair. With the scores standing at 2-2, the home fans were chanting for the final whistle when Finch broke through for the winner. Before travelling on to Cardiff, the players had a few days break at Teignmouth, which clearly had some benefits. The Cottagers played the Bluebirds to a standstill. Hammond in particular was outstanding and with two of the goals in a 3-0 win showed he had overcome a cricket injury that had been bothering him for several weeks.

An Autumnal Dip

The visit of lowly Northampton to SW6 seemed to pose few threats. For the fifth consecutive game, Fulham were unchanged and at full strength and almost 20,000 turned up expecting to see a comfortable home win. Predictably, the Cobblers spoilt the party, winning 3-1. As a spectacle, the game was ruined by the visitors' excessive use of the offside trap but this did not explain the defensive lapses which allowed Northampton to score three goals for the first time that season. Worse was to follow. At Reading a week later, Fulham conceded four goals and for the only time that season lost two games on the trot.

The shortcomings were apparent to McIntyre. Up front, Fulham had scored in every game and Newton had managed 13 in the nine games, failing to score only against Gillingham. Defensively, however, there were vulnerabilities. So the manager brought back Jake Iceton in goal (and Beecham never played for the first team again) and paid £600 for Bournemouth's full-back Joe Birch. The tough tackling ex-miner replaced Hickie and he and Iceton were both in the team for the top-of-the-table meeting with Southend at the Cottage, a game that drew a remarkable crowd of 28,757.

In a thrilling game, the re-fashioned Fulham team thoroughly deserved to share the spoils. It was a clash of styles, between the Cottagers' passing game and the Shrimpers' more direct and physical approach. The defences had the best of it. After a goalless opening 45 minutes, Fulham took the lead when Barrett headed in from Proud's corner. Southend's equaliser, from Thomson, came the same way. The closest anyone came to breaking the deadlock was when Southend's Wilson headed against his own post.

The result left Fulham in fourth place, three points adrift of Southend, with Bournemouth and Brentford in between. Amid press reports, strenuously denied by McIntyre that First Division clubs were chasing Hammond, the players and manager went to Margate for the week. The sea air seemed to agree with them because they started to find the form that would establish them as genuine Championship contenders.

Back On Track

In the next three games, Fulham took five points out of six, scoring 17 times. Clapton Orient were brushed aside 5-1 at the Cottage and in the next home game Norwich were disposed of 4-0: the nine goals were spread among six players. In between was a visit to Swindon which showed both the character in the side and how much luck is needed over a season to win a title. At half-time, the Cottagers trailed 0-2, the second coming from former Fulham striker Harry 'Abe' Morris who looked suspiciously offside. After the break, the visitors clawed their way back through Newton and Price but needed a dramatic last minute penalty save by Iceton to hold on to a point.

At the start of November, Fulham were in third place, trailing Southend and Brentford, with a tricky visit to Brighton to negotiate. The match began well for the London club. Hammond and Newton both scored in the opening 20 minutes from crosses supplied by Richards, but the ball looked out of play before he crossed for Hammond's goal. By the interval, however, Brighton were level and then wasted a golden opportunity by putting a penalty wide. In a hard-fought second half, Newton poached Fulham's winner with 20 minutes remaining. Struggling Mansfield put up

Left: Jack Finch scorer of the winner against Mansfield in November. Right: Bert Barrett.

stout resistance the following week at the Cottage. The Stags took an early lead and had an apparently good goal disallowed by the famous referee, Tom Crew. Once Finch equalised, however, Fulham piled on the pressure. But Mansfield's goalkeeper Wilson was in outstanding form, saving brilliantly three times from Newton. The visitors had yet another goal disallowed before Richards broke clear and set up the winner for Barrett. Watford, themselves in the promotion hunt, gave Fulham a jolt at Vicarage Road in the last League game of the month. The Hornets won this first of four meetings between the clubs that season relatively easily, 3-1.

After a brief diversion for the early rounds of the FA Cup (a 2-0 home win against Guildford and a 5-2 victory at Yeovil, but only after a 0-0 draw at the Cottage), Fulham continued to gather League points. First in December was a convincing 3-0 win at Bournemouth. A first minute goal by Finch and another shortly afterwards from Newton, both created by Richards, set the Cottagers on their way. A second Newton strike before the interval sealed the points. At Eastville the week before Christmas, the honours were shared. Hammond got both for Fulham while Tommy Cook, Hammond's Sussex county cricket teammate, got a brace for Bristol Rovers.

The crowded holiday schedule involved three local derbies in four days, two home games, a combined attendance of nearly 78,000, and a haul of three points from a possible six. To leave Brentford on Christmas Day morning with a point after a goalless draw was a creditable performance against the League leaders, especially as both Newton and Barrett were out with injury (Eddie Perry and Penn deputised). The Bees had won all but one of their previous 10 home games and the first v second clash attracted a new Griffin Park attendance record of 26,731. Just 24 hours later, the teams met at the Cottage for an 11.15 kick-off. Still without Newton and Barrett, Fulham scored an important win. They led through Richards at half-time and Perry scored the winner, the first of his 40 goals for the club. The margin would have been wider had Hammond not missed a penalty. A home win over QPR in a rearranged game 48 hours later would have put Fulham top of the table at the turn of the year. Despite having Newton back, they fluffed their lines. A lacklustre display allowed Rangers to take both points in a 3-1 win.

A Slow Start to the New Year

Taking into account two FA Cup ties against Watford (the replay ending in a 3-0 defeat), the Cottagers went five games, including the QPR match, without a win. Losing at Vicarage Road in the Cup mattered less than the fact Sonny Gibbon was so badly injured he did not play again that season and Barrett, back after injury, got another knock which meant he missed the next six games. The relatively inexperienced Jimmy Hindson and Paddy Molloy were drafted in by McIntyre but neither were long-term solutions.

In the first League game of the New Year, the return against Coventry, the teams followed the 5-3 scoreline at the Cottage on the opening day, with a thrilling 5-5 draw. The match swung one way and then the other with both Newton and Coventry's Billy Lake getting hat-tricks. The pitch was a quagmire and had a big influence on the game. In the last minute, Coventry were awarded a penalty but 'Clogger' Watson's spot kick got stuck in the mud and Iceton only had to pick the ball up as it rolled gently towards him to save a point.

Just two days after their Cup exit, Fulham went down to their third consecutive home defeat, to third from bottom Gillingham, one of only two teams they failed to take a single point against that season. The 2-0 defeat was the most disappointing performance and result of the season and saw the Cottagers slip to third place behind Brentford and Palace. But it proved to be a turning point.

The Tide Turns

Within 48 hours of that defeat, Fulham had another home game, a 2.30 kick-off on a Monday afternoon for a game that was originally scheduled for the FA Cup third

Jack Finch (right) and Bert Barrett (centre) help the Cottage groundman.

round day. Crystal Palace, one point and one place better off than the Cottagers, were the visitors. The awkward timing meant only 8,446 (the second lowest of the season) turned up for this vital game, which proved to be a turning point in the season. The home supporters were, however, rewarded with a comprehensive 4-0 win (with another two from Bonzo). It ended the miserable run and the start of a 14-match sequence in which only one defeat was sustained.

By the end of January, Fulham had won two more games, a 3-1 success at Luton and a 4-0 hammering of Cardiff at home. Newton was back to his best, scoring seven of his team's 11 goals in the three victories, in which only one goal was conceded. The Cottagers went into the last third of the season in second place, just one point behind Brentford.

A settled team was clearly a big advantage. In fact, nine of the players barely missed a game from the end of January until the season's climax. McIntyre made just two changes for the last 18 games, twice dipping into the transfer market to ensure the promotion was not lost. The full-back berths had been problems all season and the manager decided to switch Birch to right-back once he felt Hindson was too inexperienced to replace the injured Gibbon. The manager again went back to his old club Coventry in February and paid £750 for left-back Arthur Tilford. A more serious problem was an injury to playmaker Johnny Price which kept him out of the vital closing weeks. Again McIntyre used the chequebook, paying First Division Manchester City the sizeable fee of £1,200 for former blacksmith, Frank 'Paddy' Wrightson.

Fulham emerged from four February games with five points from a possible eight. There were two closely fought 1-0 away victories, against Northampton and Clapton Orient (Newton getting the winner on both occasions), a thrilling 3-3 draw with Reading at the Cottage and a crushing 4-1 defeat at Southend. The hard-earned point against Reading proved to be vital in May. After six straight wins in which they had scored 25 goals, the Berkshire club had emerged as strong promotion candidates. The match at the Cottage was a thriller. Fulham had to come from behind three times and needed an own goal to gain a share of the spoils.

Despite dropping three points in the month, the Cottagers gained ground. Brentford could only manage a draw and three defeats in the same period and the Bees challenge began to fade. McIntyre's men went into March three points clear at the top of the table with just 12 games remaining. Once there, they stayed there, despite some nervous performances before the title was clinched. In the final weeks of the campaign, there were some very good displays followed by a couple of inexplicable lapses, but in the end, Fulham kept their nerve and won the divisional title with a little bit to spare.

An Edgy Finale

From the crowded March programme, which included three games in four days over Easter, the Cottagers consolidated their position at the top. They escaped unbeaten from the six games and extended their lead to four points. Injuries at the start of the month forced McIntyre to give debuts to two players, who both scored vital goals but then did not play again that season. Before signing Wrightson, the manager played Albert Wood at inside-forward at home to Swindon. Signed from Sunderland the previous summer, Wood scored the equaliser in a 2-2 draw with virtually the last kick of the game. Fulham were wasteful that day, Barrett even missing a penalty, but suffered a blow when Newton was stretchered off with a neck injury. He missed the next game, with Perry again deputising, but it was another stand-in who stole the show. Frank Peters, for whom McIntyre had paid Charlton £150 that month, came in for the injured Richards for the trip to Norwich. With Fulham trailing 2-1, the debutant popped up for a timely equaliser and earn his side a point.

The Easter programme involved two games against bottom club Thames and an away trip to Mansfield. On Good Friday at Thames' West Ham Stadium, Hammond

A lovely shot of the ground from an unidentified game.

and fit-again Newton squandered early opportunities and Fulham had to settle for a goalless draw. They were relieved when the referee missed a blatant handball in the area by Birch. Goalkeeper Iceton was in top form at Field Mill the next day. An early header by Wrightson and a late strike by Richards either side of Storer's goal for the Stags secured the points for the visitors.

All the confidence returned for the Easter Monday visit of the luckless Thames. A 2-0 half-time lead became an 8-0 win at full-time. At 3-0, Thames missed a penalty and Fulham then scored five times in the last 13 minutes, Hammond completing his hat-trick with the last kick of the game. Nearest challengers Reading were keeping the pressure on, matching Fulham point for point, but never got closer to the leaders than two points.

There were just six games left at the start of April and McIntyre was able to field an unchanged team for the whole of the run in. The month began with the fourth game of the season against Watford, and the first victory, by the convincing margin of 5-0. It was a rout and when Hammond put away the fourth, it was the Cottagers 100th goal of the League campaign. Progress stalled when the Cottagers went down 2-0 at Selhurst Park. Fulham never really got going and Barrett again missed a penalty when the score was 0-0. But the other results were kind and all that was needed to secure the title was four points from the final four games.

They got the first two by beating Bournemouth 3-0 at home, all the goals the result of defensive errors. Goalkeeper Gold allowed Wrightson's speculative long-range effort to elude him for the first, a complete miss-kick presented Newton with the second and a needlessly conceded penalty allowed Newton to round off the scoring. The champagne was left on ice after the visit to Loftus Road. Rangers won 3-1 to complete the double over the leaders.

Just as in 1906 when Fulham clinched the Southern League Championship, the club's first major honour, Bristol Rovers were the opposition when the Cottagers made certain of the Third Division South title. A win was needed and they got it, but only just. The crowd of 20,454 was not the largest of the season but only at Highbury and Goodson were there bigger crowds that day. Rovers were probably the better side until they were disrupted by an injury to full-back Pickering. Fulham trailed 1-0 at half-time to Cook's goal. But, with the wind behind them and Pickering hobbling on the left wing, the home side took control. They equalised through Finch following a corner and then two goals in two minutes, headers by Barrett (from a corner) and Hammond (from a free-kick), gave then a comfortable lead although there were a few tense moments after Pickering snatched a second for Rovers when he caught Iceton napping with a low drive which curled out of the goalkeeper's arms.

The management had certainly anticipated a win. At the final whistle, a large banner saying 'Fulham Champions of Division III 1931-32' was unfurled. Skipper Len Oliver said after the game, 'Wonderful team spirit, the excellent work of our new manager and the unbounded optimism of Mr J. Dean our genial chairman have been the secrets of our success.' Of the hundreds of telegrams received by the club, none was more appreciated than that from nearest rivals Reading. It read, 'Heartiest felicitations and sincerest congratulations on your well-deserved promotion. We had good runs together and we may have many more in the future. Cordial and good wishes and good luck in every respect.' (signed) Graham, Reading.

There was still a game to play, a home match with Exeter, a formality which became a bit of a celebration. A special illustrated souvenir programme was issued costing two old pence (less than 1p today) and at the end of the game, Chairman John Dean was presented with the divisional trophy in the old Directors' Box in the Stevenage Road stand. The players did their bit, winning 3-1, the goals appropriately coming from Hammond and Newton (2).

Reflections

In his first season at the helm, McIntyre had done what he had promised the previous summer. His team topped the table by two points and a markedly superior goal average. Fulham won more games than any other club, lost fewer and scored more

Left: Jubilant supporters watch chairman John Dean receive the Third Division South shield after the final match of the season.

Right: The souvenir programme for the last game, against Exeter.

goals. Defensively, however, they were only the fourth most miserly, implying that the success was founded more on attacking flair than defensive organisation.

And in winning the title, several club records were set. The total of 111 goals and 72 at home had never been exceeded and it was not for 67 years (1998-99) that the club went through a season losing fewer than nine games. The other major record was individual. Jim Hammond's 31 League goals beat the existing club season's best of 26 (set by Sid Elliott in 1927-28) but even he was 12 short of Bonzo Newton's remarkable 43 goals in 39 appearances. Only Bedford Jezzard with 39 goals in 1953-54 has ever come close to threatening this record. Newton scored in 26 of his 39 outings, including three hat-tricks and 11 doubles. He also scored four more in five FA Cup appearances, with another treble against Yeovil. The two were the second and fourth highest scorers in the division that season (Coventry's Clarrie Burton's total of 49 is still a record for this level) and for a club to have its two leading strikers share 74 goals in a season gave the Cottagers a solid foundation for their promotion push.

There were 25 players who shared in the title win but the contribution of 13 of these amounted to fewer than 10 games. These included Beecham and Penn, survivors of relegation four years earlier, whose Fulham careers were drawing to a close, and Hindson and Perry, names for the future but who only had occasional games in 1931-32. By the halfway stage, McIntyre had found the winning blend which was only infrequently disrupted by injury and never by suspension.

The board, management and players celebrate promotion at the Holborn Restaurant.

Such was the momentum that McIntyre had created that it looked for large parts of the following season that Fulham would go straight through the (old) Second Division and bring top-flight football to the Craven Cottage end of the Fulham Road for the first time. With only a modest amount of tweaking (signing goalkeeper Alf Tootill from Wolves and two players from Southampton, full-back Mike Keeping and winger John Arnold), McIntyre's team was in the promotion hunt until the closing weeks, finally finishing third in the pre-Play-off days when only two clubs were promoted.

Summary Statistics

End	Played	Points	Position
September	8	12	3rd
October	13	18	3rd
November	16	22	3rd
December	21	28	2nd
January	26	35	2nd
February	30	40	1st
March	36	49	1st
April	41	55	1st
Final	**42**	**57**	**1st**

	H	A	Total
P	21	21	42
W	15	9	24
D	3	6	9
L	3	6	9
F	72	39	111
A	27	35	62
Pts	33	24	57

0 points v	*1 point v*	*2 points v*	*3 points v*	*4 points v*
Gillingham	Reading	Crystal Palace	Brentford	Bournemouth
Queen's Park R	Southend U	Northampton T	Bristol R	Brighton & HA
		Swindon T	Coventry C	Cardiff C
		Watford	Norwich C	Clapton O
			Thames	Exeter C
				Luton T
				Mansfield T
				Torquay U
0 points	**2 points**	**8 points**	**15 points**	**32 points**

Appearances

Goalkeeper:	Iceton 33, Beecham 9
Right-back:	Gibbon 22, Birch 14, Hindson 6
Left-back:	Birch 18, Tilford 14, Hickie 9, Bird 1
Right-half:	Oliver 39, Webb 2, Dudley 1
Centre-half:	Gibbons 42
Left-half:	Barrett 30, Penn 5, Molloy 4, Dudley 2, Webb 1
Outside-right:	Richards 33, Proud 7, Peters 1, Finch 1
Inside-right:	Hammond 32, Wrightson 10
Centre-forward:	Newton 39, Perry 3
Inside-left:	Price 31, Hammond 10, Wood 1
Outside-left:	Finch 38, Penn 4

1931-32

Division Three South — *Manager : James McIntyre*

No		Date	V	Opponents	R	H-T	F-T	Scorers	Attend
1	A	29	H	Coventry C	W	3-1	5-3	Newton 2, Barrett, Hammond 2	17,224
2	S	2	A	Exeter C	W	0-0	3-0	Newton 3	7,754
3		5	A	Gillingham	L	0-1	1-2	Richards	7,368
4		7	H	Torquay U	W	6-0	10-2	Hammond 4, Newton 2, Price 2, Finch, Proud	9,706
5		12	H	Luton T	W	1-1	3-2	Hammond, Newton, Proud	8,510
6		16	A	Torquay U	W	2-1	3-2	Hammond, Newton, Finch	5,056
7		19	A	Cardiff C	W	2-0	3-0	Hammond 2, Newton	13,233
8		26	H	Northampton T	L	0-2	1-3	Newton	19,742
9	O	3	A	Reading	L	0-1	2-4	Newton 2	11,983
10		10	H	Southend U	D	0-0	1-1	Barrett	28,757
11		17	H	Clapton O	W	0-0	5-1	Hammond 2, Price, Newton, Barrett (pen)	16,961
12		24	A	Swindon T	D	0-2	2-2	Newton, Price	4,994
13		31	H	Norwich C	W	2-0	4-0	Hammond, Finch, Newton, Richards	16,419
14	N	7	A	Brighton & HA	W	2-2	3-2	Hammond, Newton 2	10,370
15		14	H	Mansfield T	W	1-1	2-1	Finch, Barrett	16,977
16		21	A	Watford	L	0-1	1-3	Newton	14,133
17	D	5	A	Bournemouth	W	3-0	3-0	Finch, Newton 2	5,576
18		19	A	Bristol R	D	1-1	2-2	Hammond 2	5,197
19		25	A	Brentford	D	0-0	0-0		26,139
20		26	H	Brentford	W	1-0	2-1	Richards, Perry	29,253
21		28	H	Queen's Park R	L	0-1	1-3	Newton	22,236
22	J	2	A	Coventry C	D	2-1	5-5	Newton 3, Hammond, Finch	11,099
23		16	H	Gillingham	L	0-1	0-2		11,953
24		18	H	Crystal Palace	W	3-0	4-0	Hammond, Newton 2, Richards	8,446
25		23	A	Luton T	W	3-0	3-1	Newton 3	6,315
26		30	H	Cardiff C	W	1-0	4-0	Hammond, Newton 2, Richards	14,690
27	F	6	A	Northampton T	W	1-0	1-0	Newton	6,239
28		13	H	Reading	D	1-2	3-3	Hammond 2, (Richardson og)	18,730
29		20	A	Southend U	L	1-3	1-4	Hammond	6,330
30		27	A	Clapton O	W	1-0	1-0	Newton	11,014
31	M	5	H	Swindon T	D	0-0	2-2	Newton, Wood	17,555
32		12	A	Norwich C	D	1-2	2-2	Finch, Peters	11,756
33		19	H	Brighton & HA	W	0-0	3-0	Finch, Hammond, Wrightson	20,460
34		25	A	Thames	D	0-0	0-0		4,867
35		26	A	Mansfield T	W	1-1	2-1	Wrightson, Richards	5,910
36		28	H	Thames	W	2-0	8-0	Hammond 3, Richards 2, Finch, Newton 2	19,875
37	A	2	H	Watford	W	3-0	5-0	Finch, Newton 2, Hammond 2	22,590
38		9	A	Crystal Palace	L	0-1	0-2		21,326
39		16	H	Bournemouth	W	1-0	3-0	Wrightson, Newton 2 (pen)	14,544
40		23	A	Queen's Park R	L	0-1	1-3	Hammond	21,572
41		30	H	Bristol R	W	0-1	3-2	Finch, Barrett, Hammond	20,454
42	M	7	H	Exeter C	W	1-1	3-1	Hammond, Newton 2	15,502

Apps
Goals

				FA CUP					
1	N	28	H	Guildford	W	1-0	2-0	Hammond 2	12,000
2	D	12	H	Yeovil & Petters U	D	0-0	0-0		15,196
R		17	A	Yeovil & Petters U	W	1-1	5-2	Newton 3, Price, Richards	8,004
3	J	9	A	Watford	D	0-0	1-1	Newton	15,978
R		14	H	Watford	L	0-1	0-3		23,113

Gibbon	Hickie	Oliver	Gibbons	Barrett	Richards	Hammond	Newton	Price	Penn	Webb	Proud	Finch	Iceton	Birch	Bird	Dudley	Perry	Hindson	Molloy	Tilford	Wood	Peters	Wrightson	Keen	No.
2	3	4	5	6	7	8	9	10	11																1
2	3		5	6	7	8	9	10	11	4															2
2	3		5	6	7	8	9	10	11	4															3
2	3	4	5	6		8	9	10			7	11													4
2	3	4	5	6		8	9	10			7	11													5
2	3	4	5	6		8	9	10			7	11													6
2	3	4	5	6		8	9	10			7	11													7
2	3	4	5	6		8	9	10			7	11													8
2	3	4	5	6		8	9	10			7	11													9
2		4	5	6		8	9	10			7	11	1	3											10
2		4	5	6	7	8	9	10				11	1	3											11
2		4	5	6	7	8	9	10				11	1	3											12
2		4	5	6	7	8	9	10				11	1	3											13
2		4	5	6	7	8	9	10				11	1	3											14
2		4	5	6	7	8	9	10				11	1	3											15
2		4	5	6	7	8	9	10				11	1		3										16
2		4	5	6	7	8	9	10				11	1	3											17
2			5		7	8	9	10	6			11	1	3		4									18
2		4	5		7	8		10	6			11	1	3			9								19
2		4	5		7	8		10	6			11	1	3			9								20
2		4	5		7	8	9	10	6			11	1	3											21
2		4	5		7	8	9	10	6			11	1	3											22
		4	5			8	9	10	11			7	1	3		6		2							23
		4	5		7	8	9	10				11	1	3		6		2							24
		4	5		7	8	9	10				11	1	3				2	6						25
		4	5		7	8	9	10				11	1	3				2	6						26
		4	5		7	8	9	10				11	1	3				2	6						27
		4	5		7	8	9	10				11	1	3				2	6						28
		4	5	6	7	8	9	10				11	1	2						3					29
		4	5	6	7	8	9	10				11	1	2						3					30
		4	5	6	7	8	9					11	1	2						3	10				31
		4	5	6		8		10				11	1	2			9			3		7			32
		4	5	6	7	10	9					11	1	2						3			8		33
		4	5	6	7	10	9					11	1	2						3			8		34
		4	5		7	10	9			6		11	1	2						3			8		35
		4	5	6	7	10	9					11	1	2						3			8		36
		4	5	6	7	10	9					11	1	2						3			8		37
		4	5	6	7	10	9	8				11	1	2						3					38
		4	5	6	7	10	9					11	1	2						3			8		39
		4	5	6	7	10	9					11	1	2						3			8		40
		4	5	6	7	10	9					11	1	2						3			8		41
		4	5	6	7	10	9					11	1	2						3			8		42

Gibbon	Hickie	Oliver	Gibbons	Barrett	Richards	Hammond	Newton	Price	Penn	Webb	Proud	Finch	Iceton	Birch	Bird	Dudley	Perry	Hindson	Molloy	Tilford	Wood	Peters	Wrightson	Keen	
22	9	39	42	30	33	42	39	32	9	3	7	39	33	32	1	3	3	6	4	14	1	1	9	-	A
-	-	-	-	5	8	31	43	4	-	-	2	11	-	-	-	-	1	-	-	-	1	1	3	-	G

Gibbon	Hickie	Oliver	Gibbons	Barrett	Richards	Hammond	Newton	Price	Penn	Webb	Proud	Finch	Iceton	Birch	Bird	Dudley	Perry	Hindson	Molloy	Tilford	Wood	Peters	Wrightson	Keen	
2		4	5	6	7	8	9	10				11	1	3											1
2			5	6	7	8	9	10				11	1	3									4		2
2		4	5		7	8	9	10	6			11	1	3											R
2		4	5	6	7	8	9	10				11	1	3											3
		4	5		7	8	9	10	6			11	1	3					2						R

The Championship Squad: 1931-32

Jake Iceton: Signed as a 26-year-old from non-League football, goalkeeper Iceton had failed to make the grade with Hull but was the Cottagers first choice for two seasons. Brave and agile given his size, Iceton made 99 appearances for Fulham before losing out to Alf Tootill in the autumn of 1932. He left for Aldershot in May 1935 and later played for Orient. He died in his home town of West Auckland in 1981 aged 77.

Sonny Gibbon: Right-back Gibbon had won an amateur cap for Wales while playing for Merthyr, where his father was chairman. He moved to Aberdare in 1928 and then Fulham in 1929. He had made 72 consecutive appearances before injury ended the run and his season in January 1932. A boisterous character, Gibbon frequently clashed with the club management but was tragically killed in a motor cycle accident near Deal in April 1935. He was just 25.

Joe Birch: A solidly built, tough tackling but speedy full-back, Birch found his way to Fulham from Bournemouth when the promotion season was in its third month. Midlands–born Birch played just once for Birmingham before switching to the south coast where he was unable to get a regular game. McIntyre thought he would fill the awkward full-back slot, and so it proved. In seven seasons at the Cottage, he made 195 appearances and was awarded a testimonial against QPR in April 1937. Birch spent the final pre-war season with Colchester, where he lived until his death in 1980 at the age of 76.

Len Oliver: Captain of the title-winning side and a famous Fulham name, Oliver's 434 League and Cup games between 1924 and 1935 puts him seventh on the club's all-time appearances list. A one-club man (he was signed from amateurs Tufnell Park), Oliver was capped by England in 1929 when a Third Division player. A very classy wing-half and natural leader, he was highly regarded by Fulham chairman John Dean and employed in the club offices on retirement. He left under a cloud in 1938, however, and never returned to first class football. During the war, Oliver was a PE instructor and he died at his home in Letchworth in 1967 aged 62.

Syd Gibbons: Nicknamed 'Carnera' after the world heavyweight boxing champion of the day, Gibbons was a big man in every respect. Despite an impressive schoolboy career, he failed to make the breakthrough at Manchester City and moved to Fulham in May 1930. He was an immediate success and for seven seasons, and 318 games, was an automatic choice until injuries got the better of him. A powerful centre-half who loved to get forward (he once scored a hat-trick in a Second Division match, all from open play), Gibbons all-action style made him a crowd favourite. After the war, he ran a tobacconists in Putney and scouted for Fulham when he died aged 46 from a heart attack after collapsing on Putney Bridge in 1953.

Bert Barrett: In many ways, Barrett's career paralleled that of teammate Oliver. Bert played 419 times for Fulham between 1925 and 1936 and, like Oliver, was capped for England in 1929 while playing in the Third Division. A schoolboy and amateur international, he was briefly with Southampton and West Ham before signing for Fulham in 1925. Although he had been out of football for a while, he was rumoured to have been a contender for the Fulham manager's job when Jack Peart died in 1948. By then, however, Barrett had qualified as an accountant and worked for a wholesale firm in Romford Market before emigrating to South Africa in 1954. It was there that he died in 1989 at the age of 86.

Bill Richards: Very early in his Fulham career, manager McIntyre went back to his previous club, Coventry, to sign winger Billy Richards. Born in Abercanaid in 1905, this fast, tricky winger was working down the mines and playing as an amateur for Merthyr before moving on to Wolves in 1926 and Coventry in 1929. Not as prolific a scorer as his predecessor Jimmy Temple, Richards' crosses from the right nevertheless provided an invaluable supply line for strikers Hammond and Newton. Despite winning an England Junior cap in 1928 while at Molineux, he became the first Fulham to play for Wales when he was part of the side which beat Ireland 4-1 in December 1932. After 82 games and 15 goals, Richards was transferred to Brighton in 1935 and ended his League career with Bristol Rovers. He was only 51 at the time of his death in Wolverhampton in 1956.

Jim Hammond: The Championship season was Hammond's fourth at Fulham. Hove-born, he was county player at 16 and an England amateur international with Lewes in 1928 and working as a clerk in a Brighton wine office. Nicknamed the 'Galloping Hairpin', Hammond formed a lethal partnership with Newton, both of them breaking the club's scoring record in 1931-32. He was 12th man for England in the famous international with Austria at Stamford Bridge in 1932. Hammond went on to become the first Fulham player to score 100 and 150 goals for the club. His final total was 151 when injury ended his career in 1938. He played county cricket for Sussex in the summer (over 4,000 runs and 428 wickets in 196 county matches) and in 1961 was appointed a first-class umpire. He was living, as he always had, in Sussex (Hove) when he died, aged 77 in 1985.

Frank Newton: Signing Newton from Stockport for just £575 in May 1931 was a master stroke by McIntyre. In his first season, he scored a club record 43 League goals and spearheaded the promotion push. Before injury cruelly ended his career in December 1934 at the age of 32, he had scored 81 goals in 88 appearances, a remarkable rate of a goal every 97 minutes. From a family of 19 children, Romiley-born Newton found his way to Stockport via army and police service in India, where he also excelled at rugby, hockey and boxing. A typical old-fashioned bustling centre-forward, he scored 93 times in 101 outings for Stockport. But he also effectively ended McIntyre's career when the manager was sacked for selling him to Reading for just £650 and replacing him with Arsenal's Jack Lambert at £2,500, who proved a flop. Although the new manager, Jimmy Hogan, re-signed Newton, it was short-lived because he broke his leg within months and never played again. Bonzo spent his later years in the Tameside area, where he died, aged 75, in 1977.

Johnny Price: Wearing number 10 and providing the craft in the forward line was Johnny Price. Born in Mhow in India, Price had signed for Fulham in June 1928 after a non-League career with Woking that won him three England amateur caps. After impressing in his first season as a schemer or playmaker, he had a full England trial in 1929 and toured South Africa with the FA that summer. He modelled himself on Arsenal's Alex James and was a consistent performer until injuries took their toll by the mid-1930s. In total, he played 205 times for Fulham and scored 53 goals. Price was also a greyhound enthusiast, owning several dogs. He played briefly for Port Vale and coached Wimbledon and Yiewsley after the war. He was assistant secretary at Fulham for a while in the early 1960s. Price died in Southsea at the age of 83 in June 1987.

Jack Finch: Another one-club man, the versatile Finch was the only player to appear in every season throughout the 1930s. A former motor mechanic and bus driver, he signed from Walthamstow Avenue in November 1930 and made his debut weeks later. He was still in the side 294 games and 51 goals later in 1939. His build (he was just 5ft 7in tall) and pace made him a natural winger and he played on both flanks. Later in his career, he was also used as an inside-forward. Finch played on in the war years for the club and subsequently coached in Iceland and worked as a free-lance reporter in West Ham. He spent his retirement years in Worthing until his death aged 84 in 1993.

2.

The Unexpected Champions: 1948-49

Background

Since the near miss in 1932-33, Fulham had done little to suggest they were going to make the jump into the (old) First Division. In the six remaining inter war seasons and the two campaigns following the resumption of League football in 1946, the Cottagers were a consistent mid-Division Two side with top-flight football in west London confined to Stamford Bridge and Griffin Park. Even after the first few games of 1948-49, promotion seemed a remote possibility. Indifferent results followed in the wake of a major upset behind the scenes and it was not until the turn of the year that the club's chances of stepping up a grade were given any serious thought. But a marvellous second half of the season put the Cottagers in the thick of the promotion race, which went right down to the wire. In the end, they emerged triumphant and on the final day of the season celebrated the club's finest hour.

Yet there were some signs that Fulham's fortunes were looking up. The previous season, the Cottagers had won more games away from home (9) than at home (6) for the first time. In addition, they had won a famous FA Cup victory at First Division Everton. Slowly, a new team was emerging. At full-backs, there were two survivors of the pre-war era, Joe Bacuzzi, an England wartime international and rated one of the best defenders in the country, and Harry Freeman. Following an injury to Jack Watson on Christmas Day 1947, left-half Jim Taylor switched to centre-half and was so successful that he went on to win full England caps. This move allowed skipper Pat Beasley, an England international and pre-war veteran of the great Arsenal teams, to drop back from inside-forward to wing-half. Beasley had lost his pace, but playing a more defensive role made best use of his considerable control and distribution, tactical nous and leadership skills. The midfield running was left to a wartime discovery and human dynamo, Len Quested. This half-back line, the engine room of the team, came together towards the end of the previous season.

Upfront, Bob Thomas, a £4,000 signing from Plymouth the previous year, had proved a success at inside-forward in his first season. He worked well with young Arthur Stevens, a winger or centre-forward, who had signed in 1943 and went straight into the side in 1946-47. And, in the summer of 1948, Fulham paid a club record fee of £12,000 to Bournemouth for left-winger Jack McDonald. A dour personality, Yorkshire-born McDonald had begun with Wolves in 1937 and had guested for Chelsea during the war and, at the age of 27, was at or near his peak.

For all this, however, there were still weaknesses. Goalkeeper Ted Hinton, although an Irish international, was too prone to error and rather inconsistent. Since the controversial sale of Ronnie Rooke to Arsenal in December 1946, the Cottagers had lacked a natural centre-forward. Doug McGibbon had been signed from Southampton in January 1947 but despite scoring a hat-trick on his debut (as Rooke had done before him), failed to fill the gap. Next to have a go was Jimmy Jinks, bought from Millwall. He was over 30 and had lost his best years to the war and was not the answer. And the other inside-forward slot was up for grabs with the workmanlike Ayres struggling to capture the form he had shown in the reserves.

So when the team travelled to Grimsby for the first game in August 1948, some of the pieces of the jigsaw were in place. In the typical language of the time, the manager said in the programme for the first home game, 'I think that Fulham can really look forward to the coming season with more than ordinary gusto.' He proved to be right but sadly never knew it because within a week of writing those comments, the club was rocked by the sudden death of the manager.

Mourning at The Cottage

Since 1935 Jack Peart had been the Fulham manager and his 12-year stint in the job not only ended a decade of managerial instability at the club but he had successfully navigated the difficult war years. An old-fashioned administrator rather than tacti-

The Championship team. Back row, left to right: Eddie Perry (coach), Freeman, Quested, Flack, Taylor, Bacuzzi, Beasley, Frank Penn (trainer). Front row: Lewin, Stevens, R. Thomas, Rowley, S. Thomas, McDonald, Bewley.

cian or coach, Peart was a straightforward, plain speaking disciplinarian who had done his apprenticeship at Rochdale and Bradford City. His years are Fulham were unexceptional and his major achievement, taking the club to the FA Cup semi-final, occurred in his first season. Towards the end of 1947-48 he was taken ill and needed surgery but was fit enough to resume at the start of the next season. In the first week of 1948-49, however, he was back in St Mary's Hospital, Paddington and died, a month short of his 60th birthday, on 2 September.

His death was unexpected and the club was unprepared. It fell to Frank Penn and Taffy O'Callaghan, two former players now trainers, to hold the fort while the search began. Other ex-players were mentioned as likely candidates, in particular Bert Barrett and Johnny Price, two of the stars of the 1932 Third Division South winning side. In the end, it was another old player, from an earlier period who got the job.

South Africa-born Frank Osborne had come to England with his family in 1911 and 10 years later signed for Fulham from amateurs Bromley. A centre-forward or winger, he made 70 appearances for the Cottagers before a transfer to Spurs in January 1924 for a Fulham record fee of £3,000. He had also played twice for England, against Northern Ireland in 1922 and France in 1923, so becoming the first Fulham player to be capped by England. Osborne made 219 appearances at White Hart Lane and then ended his playing career at Southampton. On his retirement, he took a job with the Fulham chairman John Dean's company, Deans Blinds, and in 1935, with the special permission of the FA, was made a director of the Cottagers. To become manager, therefore, he stepped down from the boardroom (again requiring special permission) and thus completed a unique trilogy of roles with the club.

From the start, the 52-year-old Osborne took the title of General Manager and he was to remain in some sort of managerial/secretarial role until his retirement at the age of 68 in 1964. His remarkable Fulham career spanned 43 years but from the day he left until the day he died (in March 1988), he never again set foot in the Cottage. Early in his managerial term, he brought in Fulham's former centre-forward Eddie Perry as team manager and the two guided the club through to the Championship win seven months later.

New manager Frank Osborne.

An Indifferent Start

Up to the time of Peart's death, the team had shown some promise. In the opening game, they travelled to meet newly-relegated Grimsby and, on a blazing hot summer's afternoon, stunned the Mariners with a three-goal first half blitz. Jinks headed the first from a cross from the other new boy, McDonald, and Ayres and Thomas increased the margin before the break. Although goals by Clifton and Cairns reduced the arrears, Fulham were good value for their win. But it came at a cost, injuries to Bob Thomas and McDonald keeping them out of the midweek home game against Barnsley. After the win at Blundell Park, this proved a bit of a let down for the 21,000 fans. Freeman fouled Tykes left-winger Kelly and Baxter scored from the spot. It took a horizontal header by Stevens with only 15 minutes remaining to salvage a point.

The Cottagers got back to winning ways against Nottingham Forest days later at home. Jinks scored twice either side of a brace by Stevens and the game was over by half-time. Forest's star man was goalkeeper Walker who kept the score down even though Fulham eased up in the second half. Next was the return with Barnsley and 90 minutes of football at Oakwell produced the same result as at the Cottage. Griffiths scored for the home side in the first minute and it took Fulham until midway through the second half to break down a resolute home defence. McDonald earned the point directly from a 25-yard free-kick.

Just 24 hours later came the news of Peart's death and with it a run of poor results. Fulham lost four and drew one of the next six games before Osborne's appointment and, by the end of September, they had slipped to 17th in the table with almost a quarter of the fixtures completed. The first defeat of the season came at Gigg Lane a couple of days after the manager's passing. Unbeaten Bury were too good for Fulham and Kilshaw in particular gave Bacuzzi a torrid time. He set up the first for Dolan before the break and Massart scored the clincher 12 minutes from time. The Cottagers misery was completed when McDonald's late penalty kick went straight at goalkeeper Bradshaw.

A midweek home match with Southampton provided the only win in this sequence and, come the following May, it proved to be a very valuable two points. In the first half, Fulham totally dominated but had only a 30-yard pile-driver by Stevens after 30 minutes to show for their efforts. Saints Scottish international goalkeeper Ian Black (who was to join Fulham two years later) kept his side in the game with several outstanding saves. In the second half, however, the tide turned and the visitors were clearly the better side but could not break down a solid defence, in which Freeman and Taylor were commanding, to get the equaliser their play deserved.

While speculation continued on the new manager, the team were beaten twice on their travels in four days, the only time that season they suffered back-to-back defeats. At Plymouth, Bob Thomas captained the team against his old club but once Argyle had scored twice in the first seven minutes through Strauss and Squires, there was no way back. Squires added a third a minute before half-time and although Fulham had more of the play in the second half, their only consolation was

Thomas' last-minute goal. Days later, Saints got their revenge with a comfortable 3-0 win at the Dell. Day got the only goal of the first half but two Wayman strikes in the final 20 minutes gave a more realistic reflection of the balance of play.

Any hopes the Cottagers had of redeeming themselves at home to Blackburn were wasted in a scrappy match. The forward line was inept and it took a 37th minute own goal by Rovers' Eckersley, who deflected a speculative Harry Ayres effort past his own 'keeper, to give them a slim half-time lead. But midway through the second half, the old warrior Dennis Westcott equalised. The miserable sequence continued at Cardiff the following week in front of a crowd of over 38,000. An error by Hinton in the first minute gave Hullett the chance to open the scoring for the home team. The same player doubled his side's advantage with a header after 25 minutes. In the second half, Fulham seemed to get going, and, with the Cardiff defence appealing for offside, McDonald raced through to score. But for all their late pressure, Fulham could not force an equaliser and a miserable September ended with just four points from a possible 14.

The New Man Takes Over

QPR were the visitors for Frank Osborne's first game at the helm, and this first meeting between the west London neighbours since 1932 attracted a crowd of 38,667. And there were changes. The previous week a 21-year-old inside-forward had made his debut, and Osborne kept him in the side in place of Ayres. Bedford Jezzard had signed from Watford three months earlier and was to become one of the most important personalities in Fulham's post-war history. Out too went Jinks, with Stevens moving from the wing to centre-forward and Welshman Sid Thomas coming in on the flank. And in goal, Osborne gave a chance to Doug Flack who had been at the club since pre-war days but had never played in the first team.

Osborne got off to an ideal start. Bob Thomas was on the mark after only five minutes, the only goal of the first period. Hampered by an injury to left-half Albert Smith, who eventually had to leave the pitch, Rangers' 10 men were overwhelmed in the second half. Thomas added his second and Stevens got his first League hat-trick to round off an emphatic 5-0 win. Another home game followed, against top-of-the-table West Brom. Fulham lost for the only time at home in the League that season, but the match proved to be significant for the most unexpected reason. Albion won 2-1, deservedly, and came from behind to claim the points. Thomas had given the home side a third-minute lead after a 40-yard run but the inevitable equaliser came from Haines four minutes before half-time. Immediately on the re-start, Barker got

Bob Thomas scores against QPR in October 1948.

what proved to be the winner. But for Osborne, the significance was the performance of the Baggies reserve centre-forward. Arthur Rowley was only playing because Jack Walsh was on international duty for Ireland but his impressive leadership of the forward line had not gone unnoticed by the Fulham manager.

As Osborne got used to the manager's office and Perry arrived to supervise team affairs, Fulham went on a seven match unbeaten run which saw them climb to fourth place in the table by the beginning of December. It was a largely settled team with nine players playing in each of the seven games and two others playing in six, the only two changes forced by injury. The run started at Chesterfield, an 18th minute Bob Thomas goal and a resolute defensive display settling the outcome. Then Lincoln (2-1) and Coventry (1-0) were beaten at the Cottage in between which the Cottagers went to Hillsborough and beat Wednesday 2-1, with Bedford Jezzard scoring the winner, the first of his 155 goals for the club. But it was Flack who won the plaudits. Against Lincoln, he saved a penalty with just two minutes to go and Fulham leading by a single goal. And a week later, against Sheffield Wednesday, he did the same again. This time it was virtually the last kick of the game and although Witcomb scored from his first spot kick, an encroachment meant he had to re-take it. Flack saved the second effort, and a point.

Bottom-of-the-table Coventry proved a hard nut to crack at the Cottage. Although Fulham went ahead after just eight minutes when Jezzard converted a McDonald cross, they owed their win to a solid defensive performance, especially from the consistent Taylor. Leeds ended the four-match winning run. In a finely balanced game at Elland Road, the home side broke the deadlock in the 56th minute when Browning scored with a header. Bob Thomas equalised three minutes later and that completed the scoring. There was another evenly-balanced thriller the following week when Leicester visited the Cottage but this time, Fulham shaded it and took both points. Again it was Bob Thomas who made the decisive strike, another fierce shot after one of his long runs. But Fulham owed a lot to goalkeeper Flack and to the generosity of the visitors' centre-forward Don Revie who missed a sitter.

Some momentum was lost when the game at Brentford was postponed because of fog and rescheduled for April. So the Cottagers had a fortnight's break before taking on Spurs at home at the beginning of December, a match that attracted a crowd of 36,247. Tottenham, playing in red shirts and blue shorts, had the better of early exchanges and it was no surprise when they took the lead on 20 minutes through a Billy Nicholson drive. With just three minutes left full-back Freeman equalised with an astonishing 35-yard shot which flew past the groping Ditchburn. The ball hit the underside of the bar and it was the linesman rather than referee who said it had crossed the line. Curiously, Freeman had scored a similar goal against Ditchburn two years earlier. Shortly before the equaliser, Spurs' centre-half, Vic Buckingham (a future Fulham manager) headed a Stevens shot off the line. It was a thrilling derby and in the end a point won for Fulham rather one dropped.

The Turning Point

As the busy Christmas season approached, Osborne could be reasonably satisfied with his early months in office. The team had climbed from the bottom half of the table to within striking distance of the leaders, fourth behind West Brom, Southampton and Spurs. Yet, as the display at Upton Park the week after the Spurs match showed, something was still missing. West Ham deservedly won a dull London derby 1-0. The Hammers had 75 per cent of the play and should have scored more than Wright's headed goal from Woodgate's corner midway through the second half. The fact they did not was down to some resolute defending with Flack, Freeman, Bacuzzi and Taylor at their very best.

Once Jezzard shot wide with only goalkeeper Gregory to beat after five minutes, little was seen of the Fulham forwards. Stevens in particular seemed uncomfortable in the centre-forward role and the forward line, not for the first time, seemed to lack cohesion and punch. Only two teams in the top half of the table had scored fewer than Fulham's 27 goals after 19 games. The manager recognised this and moved to fill the gap. His response was a masterstroke and the turning point in the season.

When West Brom won at the Cottage two months earlier, their best player was reserve centre-forward (George) Arthur Rowley, brother of Manchester United's Jack. The win over Fulham had been Rowley's only first team outing of the season and the following week he was back in Albion's reserves. When Osborne proposed a straight swap of Rowley for Fulham's reserve winger Ernie Shepherd, who had lost out to Jack McDonald, it suited all parties. Rowley went straight into the team, with Stevens going back to the wing and Sid Thomas stepping aside. (Later in the season, Shepherd was transferred to Hull in Division Three North. In May, all three of the clubs for which he played that season, Fulham, West Brom and Hull, had won promotion.)

Rowley made his debut the Saturday before Christmas and his impressive display helped Fulham complete an easy double over lowly Grimsby. Although he did not score, Rowley made a full contribution to the win. It was his clever pass that set up McDonald for the opening goal after 10 minutes, a rare header from the winger. Against the run of play, the Mariners equalised shortly before the interval with a header by Lloyd. In the second half, the Cottagers went ahead when Bob Thomas barged goalkeeper Chisholm and the ball into the net on 51 minutes and skipper Beasley made the game safe with a blistering drive from Stevens' pass. Jim Taylor, the subject of a reported £20,000 bid from Aston Villa, was again dominant at the heart of the Fulham defence.

All the pieces were now in place and the team went from strength to strength. After a hard-fought draw on a frozen pitch at Bradford on Christmas Day morning, when Stevens' late equaliser finally broke the resistance of a defiant defence in which veteran goalkeeper Farr was in inspired form, the Cottagers went on a four-match winning run.

Bradford were the first to fall in the Boxing Day return, victims of two well-taken McDonald goals, the first a ferocious 35-yard free-kick and the second, a crisp shot taken on the turn. On New Year's Day, the Cottagers were too good for relegation-threatened Nottingham Forest in torrential rain at the City Ground. The home side were hampered by an injury to captain and left-back McCall and Fulham took full advantage against 10 men. In the 71st minute, Rowley opened his account for his new club, heading in Freeman's centre, and five minutes from time, McDonald sealed a very efficient victory.

For once, the FA Cup was a real distraction and losing at home to Third Division Walsall to a goal four minutes into extra-time was a shock but not necessarily an unwelcome one. With 18 games remaining, four clubs were the major contenders in the Second Division promotion chase. Southampton and West Brom led the way with 33 points with Spurs and Fulham, both with a game in hand, hard on their heels with 30.

Fulham displayed their promotion credentials in the two remaining January matches, both at home, when they stepped up a gear and scored 13 goals. Bury were crushed 7-2. Rowley got a first-half hat-trick, and although the Shakers had twice equalised, they were overwhelmed in the second half. Rowley got his fourth, Thomas and McDonald scored within a minute of each other and then Thomas added a seventh after a solo run and blistering shot. Plymouth suffered a similar fate a week later. Again Rowley notched a first half hat-trick, all three set up from the left by McDonald, and Stevens added a fourth from the penalty spot, awarded for handball. Argyle managed one in reply, also a penalty after Freeman handled. In the second half, Thomas scored against his old club and Jezzard got the sixth, a result which lifted Fulham into third place just a point behind West Brom.

Quested, Taylor and Sid Thomas training at the Cottage.

A Slight Blip

Just when everything seemed to be going so well, there were a couple of setbacks in February. A late goal by Fenton gave Blackburn both points at Ewood Park as the Rovers defence contained Fulham's forwards with relative ease. After an interval for a friendly at home to First Division Preston (which Fulham won 1-0), the Cottagers recovered with a 4-0 home win over Cardiff. It was all over by half-time. Jezzard opened the scoring, Stevens added a second from the penalty spot when Rowley, who looked really sharp, was floored in a goalscoring position, and a powerful ground shot by Thomas made it 3-0 before the teams turned round. Just 10 minutes into the second half, Thomas got his second following an astute pass by Jezzard and at 4-0, Fulham took their foot of the pedal and coasted to victory.

But they slipped up again the next week, at Loftus Road against a Rangers side that had not won since Boxing Day. Fulham looked uncharacteristically jittery and disorganised. When Ramscar scored with a precision header midway through the first half after a corner, even Fulham's normally tight defence looked exposed. Despite stepping up the pressure on Rangers in the second half, Flack in the Fulham goal was called into action more often than Allen in the other goal and the Cottagers could have few complaints about the result.

Going into March with just 13 games left, Fulham were in fourth place and faced the prospect of a trip to the Hawthorns to meet third placed West Brom, the only team to have won at the Cottage. The positions at the top were very tight with four clubs realistically pushing for two promotion places (and no Play-offs in those days).

	Played	Points
Southampton	30	42
Tottenham H	30	37
West Bromwich A	28	37
Fulham	29	36
Chesterfield	30	32

The meeting between the clubs in third and fourth places would have a crucial bearing on the outcome of the title and promotion positions and a win was vital to both, but probably more so to Fulham than Albion. A draw would be of most benefit to Southampton, the other main challengers. The weather conditions were appalling. The game was played on a bone-hard pitch and in a driving snowstorm but 27,595 hardy souls saw a thrilling encounter with a dramatic finale.

The Cottagers, who had never won at the Hawthorns, got off to the worst possible start. After only nine minutes, goalkeeper Flack misjudged a speculative effort by Albion's winger Elliott and the ball slipped from his grasp and over the line. In what developed into a war of attrition, Fulham limited the home forwards the single goal by half-time. They then had to play the second half with a gale force wind in their faces, adding to the problems caused by the snow. With 20 minutes of the half played, the dynamic Quested, whose boundless energy made no concession to the conditions, collected a Stevens pass and drove the ball through a cluster of defenders past the unsighted goalkeeper Saunders (who had guested for Fulham during the war). With both sides going for the win, and knowing the next goal would probably clinch it, the balance tilted in Fulham's favour. But they left it very, very late. There was no more than a minute left when Rowley, the man Albion let go in December, won a 50-50 challenge with Barlow in midfield. He ploughed his way through the snow towards the goal, fending off tackles by Vernon and Millard and drove the ball out of the 'keeper's reach for a sensational goal that deserved to win any match.

A Thrilling Climax

The win at the Hawthorns removed any lingering doubts about Fulham's promotion credentials and gave the players the belief in themselves that the prize of top-flight football was within their grasp. The team now virtually picked itself and right up to the final three games, when a minor crisis arose, Osborne was lucky with injuries. In the 10 games up to Easter Monday, only Jezzard (three games), Freeman (three games) and Quested (one game) were missing but in Ayres (one game), Sid Thomas (two games), Dave Bewley (one game) and Ron Lewin (three games) the manager could call on experienced and capable replacements.

A sense of anticipation was also building among supporters and the home crowds started to get bigger. The average for the season was 29,327, the highest in the club's history, and much of this was accounted for by the rising attendances as the prospect of promotion increased. On Easter Monday, 35,622 turned up at Cottage to see the Luton game and five days later, there were 39,149 for the visit of Brentford. There were over 41,000 for the final game against West Ham. The excitement and tension were building on the banks of the Thames as the season entered the home straight, and the supporters lifted the players to previously unimaginable heights.

Of the last 13 games from West Brom to West Ham, Fulham won nine and lost just one, a pace none of the other clubs could match. The only defeat was at the start of April at Coventry, an open, attacking clash that could have gone either way. The home side scored the only goal four minutes into the second half through debutant centre-forward Evans who got his head to a cross from right-winger Warner. Only a brilliant save by Wood prevented Rowley equalising in the last minute from a free-kick.

Before that, the Cottagers had won 3-0 at Lincoln. The game kicked off at 11.00 to avoid clashing with the running of the Lincolnshire Handicap and two first half goals (from Jezzard and Rowley) and a second from Rowley after the break sealed the points. A home draw in a bad-tempered, foul-ridden encounter with Sheffield Wednesday followed. An early Bob Thomas goal was cancelled out when winger Kilshaw scored direct from a corner. As well as dropping a point, Fulham had Jezzard limping on the right wing at the end, an injury that kept him out for three games. Days after the Coventry defeat, there was another draw, this time goalless in the re-arranged game with Brentford. Played on a Wednesday, the Bees had two former Fulham players, Dave Nelson and Viv Woodward, and one for the future, Ron Greenwood, in their line up. It was a dull game with both defences on top and it drew the slow handclap from the near-30,000 crowd.

Without the injured Jezzard and Quested, Fulham did well to get maximum points from the visit of Leeds the week before Easter. The 1-0 scoreline hardly did justice to the Cottagers dominance. They had 14 corners to Leeds' one and it was obvious from the start that the visitors had only come for a point. The only goal came three minutes into the second half. Goalkeeper Searson made the mistake of fisting the ball straight to the feet of Rowley who accepted the easiest of chances. Fulham finished the game with 10 men after Freeman pulled a groin muscle and had to sit out the next four games.

And so to Easter, a schedule of three games in four days, home and away against Luton and a trip to Leicester. Going into the holiday programme, Fulham were in third place and Saints and Albion looked the favourites for the two promotion places.

	Played	Points
Southampton	37	51
West Bromwich A	35	47
Fulham	36	46

After the Easter fixtures, it looked rather different. While Fulham were taking maximum points from their three games, Southampton lost at home to West Ham and Bury and had just the two points from a 1-0 home win over Grimsby to show for the efforts. That goal was one of only two Saints scored in their last seven games as their challenge evaporated at the death. West Brom, on the other hand, crushed Bradford 7-1 and squeezed past Coventry 1-0 at home but lost the return by the same score. So Fulham, outsiders before Easter, were the form team after.

	Played	Points
Southampton	40	53
Fulham	39	52
West Bromwich A	38	51

Both Jezzard and Quested were back for the Good Friday home game with Luton and the team clicked into top gear straight away. Stevens and Rowley gave them a 2-0 half-time lead which would have been greater but for the agility of goalkeeper Duke, a regular guest for Fulham in wartime. Rowley and Thomas doubled the lead in the second half before the Hatters' consolation from Owen. Only future Fulham player Bobby Brennan offered any real threat to the Cottagers' sound defence.

Another convincing away win followed 24 hours later. At Filbert Street, the Cottagers put three past the relegation-threatened FA Cup Finalists Leicester, but the margin flattered them. The home side had the better of the early exchanges but a breakaway goal by Jezzard, his shot going in off a post, tilted the balance in Fulham's direction. It was not until the last 15 minutes, when Thomas headed in a McDonald cross, that the Cottagers made the game safe. Rowley's last minute goal from Stevens' pass was harsh on Leicester.

On Easter Monday, Fulham completed the hat-trick of wins with a 3-1 victory at Luton. Playing in unfamiliar blue shirts and white shorts, the Cottagers fell behind to Brennan's third minute strike. But, eight minutes later, Rowley equalised with a venomous cross shot and, two minutes later, McDonald's corner eluded everyone and went straight into the net. Although the Hatters pressed after the break, Thomas clinched the points when goalkeeper Duke could only parry Stevens' shot and the ball fell invitingly for the Fulham man.

But as welcome as the points were, Osborne was presented with a real headache after the game. Goalkeeper Flack was found to have fractured his jaw diving at the feet of Brennan and would be out for the remaining three games. With reserve 'keeper Ted Hinton also injured, the manager was forced to draft in 26-year-old

Larry Gage who had started the season as third choice. Gage had played for Fulham in wartime and for Stockport and Aldershot between 1944 and 1946. He had moved to Canada in 1947 but returned for a second spell at the Cottage in August. He was about to play his first games in the three most important matches in the club's history.

Job Done

It was so tight at the top that not even three wins in their last three games would guarantee Fulham promotion. Somebody had to slip up. For the visit of Brentford, barriers were erected in Stevenage Road to funnel spectators through the turnstiles and hundreds of youngsters were allowed inside the railings on to the cinder track as almost 40,000 people turned up for the local derby. There was an early injury scare to Rowley after a collision with Greenwood but he recovered. It was the Bees who drew first blood when the diminutive Billy Dare squeezed past Bacuzzi and Taylor to beat Gage with a cross shot. But nine minutes later, Fulham were back on terms. Stevens crossed and goalkeeper Crozier, harassed by Thomas, could only knock the ball to Rowley who scored easily.

The game was decided by a moment of controversy, with the luck going Fulham's way. In the final minute, after a thrilling encounter in which the Brentford were in no mood to do their neighbours any favours, the Cottagers got a winner. A Bacuzzi free-kick landed on the reliable head of Thomas who planted the ball past a surprised Crozier. To the Brentford defenders and most of the crowd, Thomas looked yards offside but after consulting his linesman, referee Williams gave the goal. Although the Fulham player was clearly in an offside position, the linesman had spotted that the ball had grazed the head of Bees defender Manley, thus playing him onside. Brentford stormed off in disgust as the fans poured on to the pitch after hearing Southampton and West Brom had drawn 1-1 at The Dell.

White Hart Lane is an intimidating ground for any away side, and never more so than in April 1949 when 50,133 were packed in for Fulham's final away game of the season. Without a doubt, Spurs were the better side and should have won. They had three quarters of the play and most of the chances but a combination of heroic defending (Gage rose to the occasion) and wasteful shooting kept Spurs to a 1-0 interval lead. It was a scrappy goal. In a goalmouth melee, Duquemin forced the ball over the line before Bacuzzi could clear. But the full-back was on hand to clear off the line twice and last minute tackles by Freeman, Beasley, Quested and Taylor, were all needed to prevent the home side running away with the game.

Then, as so often happens, the team under pressure strikes back. There were just six minutes left when Jezzard raced down the right flank and fired in a shot that Ditchburn could only parry back in his path. The quick thinking Fulham man spotted Thomas unmarked in the middle and rather than blast the ball towards goal crossed for 'Bob-up' to head in an improbable equaliser. The point was priceless. Southampton completed their fixtures that day with a 1-0 defeat at Chesterfield and so the draw at White Hart Lane virtually ensured Fulham's promotion. All that was at stake in the final game was the divisional title and win at home over West Ham meant it would be Fulham's Championship.

On the day, the gates were closed 15 minutes before kick-off and Fulham, Flack apart, were able to field their strongest team against the mid-table Hammers. In an unquestionably tense atmosphere, the Hammers were not going to give in easily. But Rowley settled the nerves. After half an hour, he broke loose from Walker's marking, picked up a half clearance and cracked the ball in from 30 yards. With 14 minutes remaining, Rowley was again on the mark. This time, he beat Taylor from close range after the defence had failed to clear from Thomas.

Full-back Freeman helps out goalkeeper Gage against West Ham.

Rowley's opening goal against West Ham.

Above: The programme for the title decider against West Ham.

Left: Rowley's second against West Ham.

And so, it was over. The Championship won and First Division football assured. The fans raced on to the pitch at the final whistle to celebrate. Several players, Rowley included, were carried shoulder high to the dressing room. The players and officials appeared on the balcony of the Cottage to acknowledge the cheers of the supporters. For chairman Charles Dean there was the satisfaction of taking the side to a title, just as his late father John had done 17 years earlier. The intensely superstitious Osborne, who broke his own rule and watched the closing stages of the game (but from the terraces), was generous in his tribute to Jack Peart but it was his signing of Rowley more than anything else that had secured the triumph. And from somewhere, in those days of genuine austerity, the directors conjured some champagne, a deserved celebration on an historic day.

Reflections

In the end, Fulham finished a point clear of West Brom and with two more than Southampton. No team won more or lost fewer in the Second Division that season than the Cottagers and such was the turn-around in the second half of the season that they finished as the division's highest scorers. They also had the best defensive record. So it was a well-deserved, all-round success that was on nobody's radar four games into the season when Jack Peart died.

The late manager's signing of McDonald was an important addition to the side, but more significant was the new manager's deal that took Rowley to the Cottage. He scored 19 goals in 22 League appearances and he and Thomas together (23 goals in 40 appearances) were the division's most potent strike force. The Cottagers were, however, remarkably lucky with injuries. There were eight players who played in at least 37 of the 42 games. Flack and Jezzard, moreover, both missed just three games each once they got into the side and Rowley was ever-present from the time that he signed. It was a well-balanced side that seemed to be getting better and in the summer the board made the decision to stick with the same players at the higher level. Their faith was not misplaced. But in May 1949, supporters, management and players could reflect on an unlikely but rewarding climax to a season which had begun badly on the field and sadly off it.

A civic reception for the champions.

The squad en route for Spain for a close season tour after winning the title.

Summary Statistics

End	Played	Points	Position
September	10	9	17th
October	15	17	6th
November	18	22	4th
December	23	28	4th
January	26	34	3rd
February	29	36	2nd
March	33	43	2nd
April	41	55	1st
Final	**42**	**57**	**1st**

	H	A	Total
P	21	21	**42**
W	16	8	**24**
D	4	5	**9**
L	1	8	**9**
F	52	25	**77**
A	14	23	**37**
Pts	36	21	**57**

0 points v	1 point v	2 points v	3 points v	4 points v
	Blackburn R	Barnsley	Bradford	Chesterfield
		Bury	Brentford	Grimsby T
		Cardiff C	Leeds U	Leicester C
		Coventry C	Sheffield W	Lincoln C
		Plymouth A		Luton T
		Queen's Park R		Nottingham F
		Southampton		
		Tottenham H		
		West Brom A		
		West Ham U		
0 points	**1 point**	**20 points**	**12 points**	**24 points**

Appearances

Goalkeeper:	Flack 33, Hinton 10, Gage 3
Right-back:	Freeman 37, Lewin 5
Left-back:	Bacuzzi 41, Lewin 1
Right-half:	Quested 39, Bewley 3
Centre-half:	Taylor 42
Left-half:	Beasley 39, Bewley 3
Outside-right:	Stevens 27, S. Thomas 14, Hinshelwood 1
Inside-right:	R. Thomas 37, Stevens 4, S. Thomas 1
Centre-forward:	Rowley 22, Stevens 11, Jinks 9
Inside-left:	Jezzard 30, Ayres 9, R. Thomas 2, McDonald 1
Outside-left:	McDonald 40, Shepherd 2

The Championship Team: 1948-49

Doug Flack Staines-born Flack first signed for Fulham as a 16-year-old amateur in 1936. He turned professional two years later but had to wait until 1948 to make his debut. Once in, however, he was hard to displace and was a key member of the title-winning team He held his place in the top flight until he was displaced by Ian Black in 1950. He made 55 appearances before moving on to Walsall in 1953. Flack later coached Corinthian Casuals (guiding them to the 1956 Amateur Cup Final) and worked for an aircraft instrument company. He lived in Old Coulsden in Surrey and died in 2008, aged 88.

Harry Freeman: The taciturn Freeman was a full-back with great positional play and a ferocious shot. Born in Woodstock in 1918, he signed for Fulham in 1937 and played in one pre-war League game. He was an automatic choice in the early post-war seasons and made a total of 190 League and Cup appearances before a move to Walsall in 1952. Freeman subsequently coached several non-League clubs (Dover, Ashford, Windsor and Eton and Woodstock). He went into the bakery trade later in life and was still living in Woodstock at the time of his death in 1997, at the age of 78.

Joe Bacuzzi: Full-back Bacuzzi was one of the stars of the Championship side. Clerkenwell-born to Italian parents, he had made his debut in 1937 and was a regular in the final two inter-war seasons. A very stylish defender, Bacuzzi won 13 wartime caps for England (but missed out on a full cap) and guested for both Arsenal and Chelsea against the touring Moscow Dynamo side in 1945. The popular Bacuzzi retired from playing in 1956, after 299 appearances, and one of his only two goals was Fulham's first-ever in the top flight. He was reserve team trainer from 1956 to 1965 and later worked in a factory. He was still living in Clerkenwell when he died, aged 78, in 1995.

Len Quested: A wartime discovery, Folkestone-born Quested was a huge crowd favourite with his wholehearted displays in midfield. An ungainly player who had boundless energy, Quested made the breakthrough to the first team the previous season and was the engine room of the promotion side. He won an England B cap in 1950. When he was transferred to Huddersfield in 1951 after 188 games for Fulham, the crowd never forgave manager Bill Dodgin. After six years at Leeds Road, he emigrated to Australia, where he died in 2012.

Jim Taylor: Having signed for Fulham in 1938 from his local club (Hillingdon British Legion), Taylor had to wait until 1946 for his debut. Much of this time was spent in the Royal Navy. In the early post-war seasons, he was a wing-half but when he switched to centre-half over Christmas 1947, he went on to become one of the best in the country. He was outstanding in the promotion season and held his place during Fulham's subsequent top-flight seasons, making a total of 278 appearances. The elegant Taylor played twice for England and three times for the Football League. He left the Cottage in 1953 and had a season at QPR before playing and coaching several non-League clubs (Tunbridge Wells, Yiewsley and Uxbridge). A painter and decorator by trade, Taylor was 82 when he died in 2001.

Pat Beasley: Captain of the team, Beasley was the most experienced player at the Cottage. Born in Stourbridge, he joined Arsenal in 1931 and won two League Championship medals at Highbury. He moved to Huddersfield in 1936 and played in the 1938 Cup Final and was capped for England the following year. During the war Beasley guested for a number of clubs while working at the Royal Mint and signed for Fulham in 1945. Although he was 32, it was a shrewd signing. Originally a left-winger, he moved inside and then dropped back to left-half where he controlled the game. He had just one more playing season after the title win before going into management, with Bristol City and Birmingham. He was 73 when he died in Taunton in 1986.

Arthur Stevens: A loyal one-club man, Stevens played 413 League and Cup games for Fulham, scoring 124 goals (he was only the third Fulham player to a century of goals) in a playing career that stretched to 1958. He was then a coach until 1968. He first arrived at the Cottage as an amateur in 1941, turned professional in 1943 and served in the army during the war. Stevens played centre-forward but was happier on the right wing and played in both positions in the promotion season. When he left football, he ran a grocers in Banstead and died, aged 86, in 2007.

Bob Thomas: Londoner Thomas was signed from Plymouth where his brother David was playing for the sizeable fee of £4,000 in 1947. He was good value in his five years at the Cottage, scoring 57 goals in 175 appearances. The promotion season was Thomas' best. He finished top scorer with 23 goals, relying on speed and stealth rather than physical strength. He continued his goalscoring when he moved to Palace in 1952 and then dropped into non-League in 1955. Before turning professional, Thomas worked as a copy boy at the *Daily Express* and he returned to Fleet Street when he left, with the *Financial Times*. He died in 1990 at the age of 70.

Arthur Rowley: Signing Rowley at the halfway stage of the season was the turning point of Fulham's promotion season. Wolverhampton-born, he was at Molineux as an amateur in the war but signed professional for West Brom in 1944. But with his appearances limited to just 24 in over two seasons, he jumped at the chance to move to Fulham in 1948 and started on the path that would net him a record 434 League goals in 619 games over a 20-year career. Most of these, however, were scored outside the top flight, with Leicester (1950-58) and Shrewsbury (1958-64). An accomplished cricketer, Rowley also managed Shrewsbury as well as Sheffield United and Southend. He died in 2002 aged 76.

Bedford Jezzard: After war service in the army and a spell at Watford as an amateur, Bedford Jezzard signed for Fulham in July 1948. He made his debut early in the promotion season at inside-forward and went on to become one of the major personalities at the Cottage in the post-1945 era. He was a regular in the promotion season and in the three subsequent First Division seasons but it was when Fulham dropped back into Division Two that he became a prolific scorer. Before injury ended his career in 1956, he had set a club record of 154 goals in 306 appearances. He also played twice for England. Jezzard then had a successful spell as manager (1958-64) and left Fulham and football at a time of his own choosing to run the family pub in Hammersmith. He was 77 when he died in 2005.

Jack McDonald: Manager Jack Peart broke the club's transfer record when he paid £12,000 for McDonald, Bournemouth's outside-left. The Yorkshireman had started with Wolves in 1938 but switched to the Cherries a year later, and then spent much of the war serving overseas. He made a significant contribution to the promotion success, both as a scorer (nine goals) and a provider but found it tougher at higher level. He played 78 times for Fulham before going back to the south coast, with Southampton in 1952. He finished his League career at Southend and became a schoolteacher. He was living on the Isle of Wight at the time of his death at the age of 85 in 2007.

1948-49

League Division Two   Manager : Jack Peart / Frank Osborne

No		Date	V	Opponents	R	H-T	F-T	Scorers	Attend
1	A	21	A	Grimsby T	W	3-0	3-2	Jinks, Ayres, Thomas (R)	19,271
2		25	H	Barnsley	D	0-0	1-1	Stevens	21,005
3		28	H	Nottingham F	W	4-0	4-0	Jinks 2, Stevens 2	27,822
4	S	1	A	Barnsley	D	0-1	1-1	McDonald	17,847
5		4	A	Bury	L	0-1	0-2		18,687
6		8	H	Southampton	W	1-0	1-0	Stevens	24,700
7		11	A	Plymouth A	L	0-3	1-3	Thomas (R)	24,203
8		15	A	Southampton	L	0-1	0-3		24,655
9		18	H	Blackburn R	D	1-0	1-1	Ayres	27,198
10		25	A	Cardiff C	L	0-2	1-2	McDonald	38,423
11	O	2	H	Queen's Park R	W	1-0	5-0	Thomas (R) 2, Stevens 3	38,667
12		9	H	West Bromich A	L	1-1	1-2	Thomas (R)	31,636
13		16	A	Chesterfield	W	1-0	1-0	Thomas (R)	16,488
14		23	H	Lincoln C	W	2-1	2-1	Stevens, McDonald	24,760
15		30	A	Sheffield W	W	1-0	2-1	Thomas (R), Jezzard	34,096
16	N	6	H	Coventry C	W	1-0	1-0	Jezzard	24,318
17		13	A	Leeds U	D	0-0	1-1	Thomas (R)	26,756
18		20	H	Leicester C	W	0-0	1-0	Thomas (R)	23,873
19	D	4	H	Tottenham H	D	0-1	1-1	Freeman	36,247
20		11	A	West Ham U	L	0-0	0-1		22,689
21		18	H	Grimsby T	W	1-1	3-1	McDonald, Thomas (R), Beasley	19,996
22		25	A	Bradford	D	0-1	1-1	Stevens	20,742
23		27	H	Bradford	W	2-0	2-0	McDonald 2	22,242
24	J	1	A	Nottingham F	W	0-0	2-0	Rowley, McDonald	19,791
25		15	H	Bury	W	3-2	7-2	Rowley 4, Thomas (R) 2, McDonald	19,896
26		22	H	Plymouth A	W	4-1	6-1	Rowley 3, Stevens, Thomas (R), Jezzard	29,715
27	F	5	A	Blackburn R	L	0-0	0-1		22,582
28		19	H	Cardiff C	W	3-0	4-0	Jezzard, Stevens, Thomas (R) 2	40,795
29		26	A	Queen's Park R	L	0-1	0-1		27,440
30	M	5	A	West Bromich A	W	0-1	2-1	Quested, Rowley	27,595
31		12	H	Chesterfield	W	0-0	2-1	Thomas (R) 2	29,096
32		19	A	Lincoln C	W	2-0	3-0	Jezzard, Rowley 2	13,199
33		26	H	Sheffield W	D	1-1	1-1	Thomas (R)	34,030
34	A	2	A	Coventry C	L	0-0	0-1		26,364
35		6	A	Brentford	D	0-0	0-0		29,160
36		9	H	Leeds U	W	0-0	1-0	Rowley	23,961
37		15	H	Luton T	W	2-0	4-1	Rowley 2, Stevens, Thomas (R)	35,622
38		16	A	Leicester C	W	1-0	3-0	Jezzard, Thomas (R), Rowley	34,654
39		18	A	Luton T	W	2-1	3-1	Rowley, McDonald, Thomas (R)	20,125
40		23	H	Brentford	W	1-1	2-1	Rowley, Thomas (R)	39,149
41		30	A	Tottenham H	D	0-1	1-1	Thomas (R)	50,133
42	M	7	H	West Ham U	W	1-0	2-0	Rowley 2	41,133

Apps	
Goals	

				FA CUP					
3	J	8	H	Walsall	L	0-0	0-1		32,000

Hinton	Freeman	Bacuzzi	Quested	Taylor	Beasley	Stevens	Thomas R	Jinks	Ayres	McDonald	Shepherd	Thomas S	Bewley	Jezzard	Flack	Hinshelwood	Lewin	Rowley	Gage	
1	2	3	4	5	6	7	8	9	10	11										1
1	2	3	4	5	6	7		9	10		11	8								2
1	2	3	4	5	6	8		9	10	11		7								3
1	2	3	4	5	6	8		9	10	11		7								4
1	2	3	4	5	6	7	8	9	10	11										5
1	2	3	4	5	6	7	8	9	10	11										6
1	2	3	4	5		7	8	9		10	11		6							7
1	2	3	4	5	6	7	8	9	10	11										8
1	2	3	4	5	6	7	8	9	10	11										9
1	2	3	4	5	6	9	8			11		7		10						10
	2	3	4	5	6	9	8			11		7		10	1					11
	2	3	4	5	6	9	8			11		7		10	1					12
	2	3	4	5		9	8			11		7	6	10	1					13
	2	3	4	5	6	9	8			11				10	1	7				14
	2	3	4	5	6	9	8			11		7		10	1					15
	2	3	4	5	6	9	8			11		7		10	1					16
	2	3	4	5	6	9	8			11		7		10	1					17
		3	4	5		9	8			11		7	6	10	1		2			18
	2	3		5	6	9	8			11		7	4	10	1					19
	2	3		5	6	9	8			11		7	4	10	1					20
	2		4	5	6	7	8			11				10	1		3	9		21
	2	3	4	5	6	7	8			11				10	1			9		22
	2	3	4	5	6	7	8			11				10	1			9		23
	2	3	4	5	6	7	8			11				10	1			9		24
	2	3	4	5	6	7	8			11				10	1			9		25
	2	3	4	5	6	7	8			11				10	1			9		26
	2	3	4	5	6	7	8			11				10	1			9		27
	2	3	4	5	6	7	8			11				10	1			9		28
	2	3	4	5	6	7	8			11				10	1			9		29
	2	3	4	5	6	7	8			11				10	1			9		30
	2	3	4	5	6	7	8			11				10	1			9		31
	2	3	4	5	6	7	8			11				10	1			9		32
	2	3	4	5	6	7	8			11				10	1			9		33
	2	3	4	5	6	7	8		10	11					1			9		34
	2	3	4	5	6	8	10			11		7			1			9		35
	2	3		5	6	8	10			11		7	4		1			9		36
		3	4	5	6	7	8			11				10	1		2	9		37
		3	4	5	6	7	8			11				10	1		2	9		38
		3	4	5	6	7	8			11				10	1		2	9		39
		3	4	5	6	7	8			11				10			2	9	1	40
	2	3	4	5	6	7	8			11				10				9	1	41
	2	3	4	5	6	7	8			11				10				9	1	42

Hinton	Freeman	Bacuzzi	Quested	Taylor	Beasley	Stevens	Thomas R	Jinks	Ayres	McDonald	Shepherd	Thomas S	Bewley	Jezzard	Flack	Hinshelwood	Lewin	Rowley	Gage	
10	37	41	39	42	39	42	39	9	9	41	2	15	6	30	29	1	6	22	3	A
-	1	-	1	-	1	12	23	3	2	9	-	-	-	6	-	-	-	19	-	G

Hinton	Freeman	Bacuzzi	Quested	Taylor	Beasley	Stevens	Thomas R	Jinks	Ayres	McDonald	Shepherd	Thomas S	Bewley	Jezzard	Flack	Hinshelwood	Lewin	Rowley	Gage	
	2	3	4	5	6	7	8			11				10	1			9		3

3.

The Maestro's Season: 1958-59

Background

After the three-year sojourn in the (old) First Division ended in 1952, Fulham dropped back into the Second for another seven seasons. The first five of these were very enjoyable but largely unsuccessful. Between 1952 and 1957, supporters had the privilege of watching the gifted young Johnny Haynes and talented Bobby Robson grow to maturity, as well as centre-forward Beddy Jezzard at his most dynamic. In the five seasons up to 1957 the Cottagers scored 428 goals in 210 games, an average of two a game. Of the total, 272 (2.5 per match) were scored at the Cottage. The lowest for any season was 76 in 1954-55 while the 98 they scored the previous season was the highest in the whole of the Football League.

That Fulham were never better than a mid-table side was attributable to their defence, as porous as the forwards were prolific. The Cottagers leaked goals, 390 in the same 210 games, which left them becalmed somewhere between eighth and 14th place. But it began into change in 1957 when Dug Livingstone took over as manager.

A hugely experienced football man, Livingstone's playing career went back to Celtic and Everton in the early 1920s and his managerial jobs included spells at Sparta Rotterdam and in charge of the Belgium and Republic of Ireland sides.

Immediately prior to joining Fulham, he had steered Newcastle to FA Cup success at Wembley in 1955. An easy going, unflappable character, the 58-year-old Living-stone had to cope with the loss of two of the club's most prized assets when Robson was sold to West Brom and Jezzard's career was ended by injury in the space of a few months in 1956. He set about re-shaping the Fulham team and the work he started in 1957 bore fruit two years later.

He was very unlucky that promotion was not won a year earlier. It was Livingstone who drafted teenagers Tony Macedo and George Cohen into the first team. He also converted Roy Bentley from an inside-forward to half-back and bought full-back Jimmy Langley from Brighton and centre-forward Maurice Cook from Watford. In 1957-58, his team was going for an improbable double, an appearance in the FA Cup Final and promotion from the Second Division. They lost out in a semi-final replay to the post-Munich Manchester United and as a result of the fixture congestion that followed the Cup run (nine games in 28 days), stumbled at the last in the promotion stakes.

Much to everyone at the Cottage's surprise, Livingstone turned down the offer of a new contract in the summer of 1958, saying his wife had failed to settle in the south and so he wanted to return north. He took over at Chesterfield where he stayed until 1962. He left a solid inheritance for his successor who, with only a modest amount of tweaking, took over a side that had a promotion look about it from the start.

The promotion squad. Back row, left to right: Mullery, Cohen, Lampe, Bentley, Langley, Macedo, Hewkins, Cook, Lowe. Front row: Doherty, Leggat, O'Connell, Hill, Haynes, Key.

Re-Enter Jezzard

The board's choice to replace Livingstone was Beddy Jezzard, a familiar name to Fulham supporters. He first came to the fore as an inside-forward in the 1948-49 Second Division Championship side but had come into his own as a centre-forward in the Second Division seasons of the mid-1950s. A broken ankle sustained on a tour of South Africa with the FA in the 1956 close season ended his playing career before he was 30 but not before he had set a club record of 154 goals. Jezzard tried for a season to get back to fitness and when it was apparent he would never play again, he joined the coaching staff, taking on the youngsters in the Metropolitan League. Appointing him as manager was a bit of a gamble. Aged only 30 with virtually no management experience, he was being asked to take over a group of players who had mostly been teammates a year earlier. But he had old hands like Frank Osborne, the General Manager, and Frank Penn, the trainer, to steer him through any difficult patches. And Livingstone had left a squad in very good shape which started the season among the promotion favourites.

There was only one major change to the squad during the summer months, and it was a crucial one. Roy Dwight, a cousin of Elton John (Reg Dwight), Jezzard's successor in the centre-forward berth and top scorer in both 1956-57 and 1957-58, was sold to First Division Nottingham Forest in the summer of 1958 (and went on

New manager Bedford Jezzard.

to score in the 1959 Cup Final against Luton). Fulham went to Scotland for his replacement. Graham Leggat was an established Scottish international when he arrived at the Cottage and had played in the 1958 World Cup Finals in Sweden. His debut for Scotland was in 1956 against England at Hampden Park when he opened the scoring only for England to equalise in the dying seconds through Johnny Haynes. The college-educated Leggat was an intelligent, athletic, fast and brave winger or centre-forward who had won League and Cup honours in his five years with Aberdeen. At £16,000 he proved a superb acquisition for the Cottagers and remains today the only Fulham player to score a century of goals in the top flight.

With 21 goals in 36 games, Leggat was a resounding success in his first season but, in terms of contribution, even he had to play second fiddle to Johnny Haynes. Although still only 24 years old, this was Haynes' sixth full season in the first team and Fulham supporters had seen him blossom from teenage prodigy to the best inside-forward in the country. As captain, he was inspirational and led by example, dominating games for the whole 90 minutes. His distribution was incomparable and in Leggat he found a winger who was on the same wavelength and could make the most of his defence-splitting through passes. But in 1958-59 the Maestro added a new dimension to his game – goalscoring. For the only time in his 18 seasons, Haynes was top scorer. His personal best of 26 in 34 games included four hat-tricks and even though he went on to pass Jezzard's scoring record, he was never again as

prolific in a single season. This was unquestionably the best Fulham team in Haynes' short career but even so, he stood head and shoulders above his colleagues, majestic, imperious and a winner.

So, spirits were very positive among the players and expectations high among supporters before the season started. In its

Left: Graham Leggat scoring on his debut against Stoke.

Below: Johnny Haynes scores the first of his four goals against Lincoln in September.

usual Fulhamish way, the programme for the opening game summed it up. 'Everybody here today is saying it: "Well, what is to be this season?" It is no use asking us for the answer because we are asking ourselves the same question. All we can say is this…and it's a promise. We'll put in all we've got to try to make it an even better and more successful campaign than last.' It took just 45 minutes of the new season to show that this was not an idle boast.

A Flying Start

Fulham were fast out of the blocks and from the kick-off, were in the leading pack. They won their first six matches, the club's best-ever start and not bettered until the Tigana team of 2000, and were unbeaten until the 13th game. The Cottagers topped the table at the end of September and were never out of the top two promotion places for the rest of the campaign. In the end, they finished second, two points behind Harry Catterick's rampant Sheffield Wednesday who bounced back to the top flight at the first attempt. But Fulham were a huge seven points (only two for a win in those days) in front of Sheffield United and Liverpool in third and fourth places.

Stoke were the first to feel the force of Fulham's assault on the top. In the opening match, played in blazing sunshine at the Cottage, the home team were a goal up in the first minute. From Langley's corner, Hill headed down for Haynes to fire past the helpless Robertson. By half-time, it was 4-0, with three different scorers, a Cook header from a Cohen cross, Chamberlain finishing off a great run by Leggat, and then Leggat himself opening his account in the 41st minute from another Langley centre. In the second half, Cook completed his hat-trick, making it 6-0 and nobody in the near 32,000 crowd begrudged Stoke their goal which came from Oscroft seven minutes from time.

In many ways going to Sunderland in midweek and winning the first-ever League game at Roker Park outside the top flight was even more impressive. 'Haynes did the work of two men' said one report and the captain was instrumental in both of his side's second half goals, by Leggat (52 minutes) and Chamberlain (72 minutes). Sunderland's reply came 10 minutes from the end when a Bircham shot was deflected past Macedo by Bentley. The margin between the sides was greater than the scoreline implied, and in the midweek return seven days later, Fulham showed their superiority. Despite leading twice, Sunderland finished on the wrong end of a 6-2 hammering, which was again orchestrated by Haynes. He got a hat-trick, his first in the 35th minute equalising Kitchenbrand's fifth minute header. O'Neill restored the visitors lead after 40 minutes, but the second half was one-way traffic. Chamberlain, put through by Langley, equalised on 51 minutes before Haynes completed his hat-trick (58 and 67 minutes). Leggat (85 minutes) after another Langley run and a Langley penalty (88 minutes) after Leggat was fouled completed the rout. In between the two wins over Sunderland, was a 2-1 victory over Swansea at the Vetch. Despite being caught up in a traffic jam at Porthcawl on their way to ground, Fulham were much too good for their hosts. Haynes outshone Allchurch and he gave Fulham an eighth-minute lead, the only goal of the first half. Swansea picked up the pace in the second half and scored when a penalty was harshly awarded against Lowe. He put his hands up to defend himself from Charles' shot but the referee gave a penalty when it hit his hands. Daniel scored from the spot. In a thrilling final 10 minutes, Leggat poked home the winner after a goalmouth scramble.

New boy Leggat made quite an impact. In fact he scored in his first six matches, still a club record, and his introduction to the team was seamless. The fifth win, at home to Ipswich, was harder work, largely because Fulham were too casual. They looked to be on for another six-goal spree but allowed Ipswich to go in at half-time on level terms. In the 12th minute, after constant Fulham pressure, Town caught Langley out of position upfield and outside-right Berry broke away and crossed for Rees to slip the ball past Macedo. It took just 30 seconds for Haynes to equalise with a long-range effort but again another Ipswich breakaway and another goal, this time a header by Curtis from Leadbetter's left wing cross, the best goal of the game. That was on 28 minutes and, three minutes later, Cook nodded in a Leggat cross to level matters. After four goals in the first 30 minutes, it was nearly an hour before the next and decisive score. Inevitably, Leggat was involved. A move involving Hill and Haynes down the left gave Chamberlain and Leggat the chance to score and it was the Scotsman who scrambled it over the line.

Although they got the points, and were by far the better side, the narrow win over Ipswich should have taught Fulham a lesson about wastefulness in front of goal and complacency. They were certainly not casual days later at Lincoln when they came back from a two-goal deficit to win 4-2. The Imps got off to the ideal start with goals from Chapman and Withers but a tactical switch at half-time, Cook going out on the wing and Leggat moving inside, changed the game. It was Leggat who got Fulham back in the match after 57 minutes and Haynes equalised after 67. Thereafter it was all Fulham. Another goal was inevitable, and Leggat got it, breaking through a static Lincoln defence with eight minutes to go. Chamberlain made it safe in the last minute and stretched the 100 per cent record to six games.

That was as far as it went. A goalless draw was all the Cottagers could manage at Eastville against a well-organised Bristol Rovers side. But it could have been so different. In the third minute, Leggat was sent sprawling in the penalty area by Doyle. Langley scored from the spot but the referee adjudged that Leggat had encroached and the re-taken penalty crashed against the foot of the post. The miss gave heart to Rovers who were well worth their point.

It did not take Jezzard's men long to recover. They had three games left in September and all were won, with 10 goals scored and four conceded. In the space of three days, Haynes demonstrated his real class in home games against Lincoln and Derby. He got all four in the 4-2 demolition of Lincoln. Cook and Chamberlain were the providers of the Maestro's two first half goals. Lincoln had the temerity to equalise with two goals in 10 second-half minutes, from Harbertson and Chapman, but Haynes had something in reserve. He scored twice more, one a brilliant strike the other a fortunate tap in after the ball rebounded from a post. Against Derby less than 72 hours later, the captain's contribution was just as decisive. Despite taking a seventh-minute lead through Cook, Fulham not only trailed 2-1 at half-time (Cargill in the 17th minute and a soft shot from Mays which was fumbled by Macedo just after the half hour) but were down to 10 men in those pre-substitute days. Leggat was stretchered off with a nasty knee injury after a clash with a Derby defender in the ninth minute. But 10 minutes into the second half, Haynes took a pass from Hill on the halfway line, went past two defenders and beat the goalkeeper with a fierce shot. He did it again in the 82nd minute, another brilliant individual strike to make the final score 4-2. Langley had scored Fulham's third a minute after Haynes' first with a terrific long-range drive.

With the veteran Stevens coming in for the injured Leggat, Fulham finished the month with a 2-0 win at Leyton Orient. It was a full-blooded affair, tense, fast and hard-tackling, with Orient full-back Wright the central character. His mistake gave Chamberlain the opportunity to open the scoring from 18 yards in the third minute. He had the chance to redeem himself 15 minutes later when Stapleton fouled Julians in the area but his penalty kick was saved by Macedo. Then, on the hour, with the game still in the balance, Wright slid to clear the ball off the line only to knock it in the path of Cook who scored the clinching goal.

So, a rewarding September ended with nine wins and a draw from the first 10 games, and Fulham leading the table. In neither of the club's previous promotion seasons had they made such an outstanding start. Behind them, ominously, were Sheffield Wednesday, with 17 points. The injury to Leggat was not as serious as first feared, but in the coming couple of months, both Hill and Haynes were to be sidelined for several weeks, which strained the limited resources. And the manager was to make a significant tactical change. He switched the experienced Bentley from right-half to centre-half, a move that worked brilliantly. Bentley's wonderful footballing brain and great control and distribution were seen to best effect at the heart of the defence where his lack of pace was not exposed. Stapleton made way for him and, until February, Lawler and Lowe filled the wing-half positions.

Autumnal Wobble

Pleased as they were with the start, nobody at the Cottage believed that the team could maintain that sparkling form indefinitely. When injuries, international calls and the softer grounds started to take their toll, not to mention bad luck, points would be dropped. And for many Second Division sides, Fulham, with Johnny Haynes in the line-up, were *the* team to beat. And so it proved from October to early December. In fact, the indifferent spell continued through Christmas and it was the New Year before they re-captured the early season sparkle. Of the next 15 games played, only six were won, six were lost, the goals supply slowed and ground was lost at the top of the table to Sheffield Wednesday.

This lean spell started with a home game against lowly Scunthorpe. Without Haynes, who was on international duty, and 38-year-old Stevens deputising at inside-forward and as captain, Fulham looked decidedly lacklustre. After 90 very ordinary minutes, the Cottagers had lost their 100 per cent home record and the visitors had picked up their first away point. And to rub salt into the wound, Fulham got both goals. They went behind when a cross by Marriott was diverted into his own net by Bentley early in the second half. Just five minutes later, Leggat, who was switched from the wing to the middle, took Hill's pass and raced through to beat the stationary goalkeeper with a shot that went in off a post. There were still 36 minutes to find a winner, but for all their huffing and puffing, the Cottagers could not break down a determined defence.

Another draw at Grimsby followed a week later. With Haynes back but John Doherty in for injured Hill, Fulham fell two goals behind in the first 14 minutes, scored by Cockerill and Fell. But gradually the visitors clawed their way back into the game, inspired by their captain. Langley reduced the arrears in the 49th minute from Chamberlain's pass and after laying siege to the Grimsby goal, Chamberlain himself scored the equaliser with a shot from an acute angle after another Haynes pass. A draw was probably a fair result. For all Fulham's possession in the second half, they still needed two brilliant Macedo saves, one in the last minute, to hold on to a point.

It was unlucky 13 when Liverpool visited the Cottage, a match which stretched the win-less run to three games. In the pre-Shankly era, Liverpool played a very direct style and were not averse to strong physical challenges or spoiling tactics. Controversially, they had dropped the legendary Billy Liddell for this match, while Fulham had Johnny Key making his League debut for the injured Leggat and Tony Barton deputising for Hill. And, on the left wing, playing what proved to be the last of his 413 games was Stevens, filling in for the injured Chamberlain. Even with Haynes prompting from midfield, Fulham's makeshift forward line had little joy. For their part, Liverpool did not have a single shot on target in the first half. After the break, they played with more self-belief and five minutes from time, Liddell's replacement, Bimpson, got the only goal of the game from A'Court's cross. Stevens had two 'goals' disallowed for offside, one in each half, and so the League's last un-beaten record was gone.

Some measure of relief came the following week when Fulham got back to winning ways at Middlesbrough. Against a Boro team that included Brian Clough and Peter Taylor, and were managed by pre-war Fulham player Bob Dennison, the Cottagers showed that they had more to offer than Johnny Haynes. With Key and Barton continuing, they were 3-0 up in half an hour thanks to a brilliant Leggat hat-trick. Clough scored twice, once in each half, but Fulham stood firm. To win away was especially pleasing but to do it with 10 men for most of the game was especially satisfying. Langley had to go off after a mid-air collision with Day. The comments made by the club in the subsequent home programme about the physical approach adopted by Middlesbrough and Liverpool led to protests to the League and an apology to both from Fulham.

With the same team that beat Middlesbrough, Fulham began the second third of the League campaign with an emphatic 4-2 home win over Sheffield United. The Blades were in the promotion pack and gave a good account of themselves. They took a 39th minute lead through Hodgson which lasted less than 60 seconds. Key got a fortunate equaliser when goalkeeper Hodgkinson misjudged his swerving shot. A Haynes header from a Lowe free-kick (60 minutes) and Cook's shot from Barton's pass (75 minutes) seemed to make the game safe for Fulham but Russell pulled one back with a fine header with five minutes left. But then Leggat struck the fourth to give his side a margin of victory that flattered them. The fact that Macedo was generally rated the Man of the Match indicates that the Cottagers had to work hard for their victory.

When Fulham went to meet Bristol City at Ashton Gate, old boy Wally Hin-shelwood gave them a hard time but fortunately England striker John Atyeo was in a wasteful mood. City did score, but from an Etheridge penalty, awarded when Bentley brought down Watkins after just four minutes. Within five minutes, the Cottagers were level thanks to a superb Haynes header, the culmination of a clever three-man passing move. It was only in the final 15 minutes that Fulham stepped up a gear but found goalkeeper Cook equal to anything they had to offer.

Then there was a run of six games without Haynes, who damaged a knee playing for the Football League. With young Doherty wearing the No 10 shirt, this was a testing time and three home wins and three away defeats sounded very much like the old Fulham. The away defeats were narrowly at Huddersfield (1-2) but emphatically at Rotherham (0-4) and Stoke (1-4). For the trip to the Victoria Ground, Jezzard gave a debut to another promising youngster, Brian O'Connell, but with four reserve forwards in the team that day (only Cook of the regulars was fit), Fulham were always going to struggle.

A week earlier, there was a more spectacular debut. Charlton were the visitors, and with both Leggat and Chamberlain still on the injured list, the manager retained Barton on the right but gave a first game to Mike Johnson, a 25-year-old who was signed from non-League Gloucester the previous August but who had previously failed to make the grade at Newcastle or Brighton. On a very heavy pitch, Johnson scored two goals with blistering shots, enough to secure the points despite Lawrie's late strike for the visitors. The injury jinx struck again when Hill limped off after pulling a thigh muscle which kept him out of the next three games.

The two earlier Haynes-less home wins were over Cardiff (2-1) and Barnsley (5-2). The Bluebirds made Fulham work very hard for the points. A beautifully Leggat-created goal for Cook after 32 minutes seemed to put the Cottagers on course for a comfortable win but a slip by Macedo 20 minutes from time, when he misjudged a lob by Baker to present Walsh with a gift, set up a nervous climax. Then a cross by Doherty, a header by Cook and Chamberlain was on hand to finish. Barnsley, on the other hand, offered only token resistance. An own goal by Houghton after three minutes, when he deflected Cohen's shot, put Fulham on the road to victory. Although Kaye equalised early in the second half, goals from Leggat (2), Doherty and Cook were more than enough. Even when Graham got a second for the Tykes when the score was 4-2, the outcome was already assured.

Fulham went into the Christmas double header against Brighton in second place, with 32 points from their 22 matches, one point less than Wednesday and with a game in hand. They were three points clear of third-placed Stoke who had also played a game more. But the holiday period was overshadowed by the death of the chairman, Charles Bradlaugh Dean after a long illness. He was 65 and had succeeded his

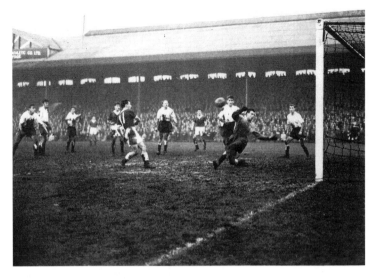

Goalkeeper
Macedo thwarts
Charlton No.11
Lawrie in the 2-1
win in December.

father (and one of the club's founding fathers, John) on his death in 1944. The family were totally committed to the club in a very Victorian, paternalistic manner. Their firm, Deans Blinds, had a page of advertising in every home programme and the company employed a number of former players as sales reps once they had retired. Although the late chairman's two sons, Tony and Charles junior, were on the board, there was no third generation of Deans in the chair. It went instead to another board member and life-long supporter, Tommy Trinder. That decision had momentous consequences for the club further down the road but, for the moment, to have a high profile entertainer as chairman was thought to be an advantage. It was certainly very Fulhamish.

On Boxing Day Fulham and Brighton served up a five-star thriller from which the Cottagers emerged 3-1 winners. They had Haynes and Leggat fit again, but it was two Brighton old boys who did the damage. First, Johnson put Fulham ahead in the 42nd minute, his third goal in his third game and then in the last five minutes, Langley fired in a fierce shot following a short corner to make it 3-1. In between, Thorne had equalised for the Seagulls in the 54th minute but Cohen restored the lead in the 66th minute, his first-ever goal. It was also the first time both Fulham full-backs scored in the same game, and both goals were from open play. But 24 hours later, the Seagulls got their own back in front of a record Goldstone Ground crowd of 36, 342. Haynes and Leggat struggled with their second game in as many days and the home side, fired up by an excited crowd, deserved their 3-0 win. Fulham seemed intimidated by Brighton's physical approach and lost out to goals by Dixon (23 and 76 minutes) and Thorne (66 minutes).

If the defeat at Brighton was a disappointment, the home defeat by Swansea in the opening game of 1959 was a real setback. Against a team in the lower half of the table, it was a game Fulham were expected to win, and in terms of possession, should have done. But, on the stroke of half-time, a one-two with Allchurch gave Palmer the chance to score the Swans opening goal. With Haynes unusually subdued (or well held by Hughes) and Hill below par, only Leggat posed a real threat to the visitors. His cross created the equaliser for Cook in the 82nd minute after constant Fulham pressure. And just when a draw seemed the most likely outcome, Allchurch

Jimmy Hill is denied.

broke down the right in the 88th minute and slipped the ball to Davies who gave Macedo no chance.

The defeat meant that not only did the gap with Wednesday widen to five points but also that the Cottagers surrendered second place to Liverpool on goal average. The intervention of the FA Cup gave Jezzard's men time to re-group. Their involvement in the competition in 1958-59 lasted four games and did not get beyond round four. It took two games to dispose of non-League Peterborough (0-0 at home and a 1-0 win at London Road courtesy of Mike Johnson) and two games for First Division Birmingham to dispose of Fulham. After a 1-1 draw at St Andrews, the Blues won 3-2 at the Cottage. But for once, the old cliché about being able to concentrate on the League had more than a ring of truth to it.

Into Top Gear

The defeat by Swansea seemed to be the wake-up call Fulham needed. Of the remaining 17 games, they lost just three, one of which came after promotion had been clinched. There were 12 wins in this sequence, including a club record eight on the trot at home. Their efforts were helped by the fact that the injury jinx eased. The only game that both Haynes and Leggat missed was at home to Huddersfield, a day when Haynes was playing for England and Leggat for Scotland at Wembley. (No postponements for international duty in those days.) And for the last 14 games, there was a third factor. Langley was unfit for the visit of Orient in February and so manager Jezzard re-shuffled his pack. He moved Lawler from left-half to left-back and switched Lowe from right to left-half. In at right-half for his League debut he brought 17-year-old Alan Mullery. Born in nearby Notting Hill, Mullery had only signed professional forms two months earlier but he made a sensational start. From that moment, he was an automatic choice until his retirement in 1976, making 412 appearances for Fulham either side of an eight-year stint at White Hart Lane. Mullers is among a handful of players (such as Haynes, Bobby Robson, Tony Gale and Gordon Davies) who made an immediate impact and then went on to carve out a special niche in club history.

A last minute goal by Haynes against 10-man Ipswich gave the Cottagers a 2-1 away win and got the promotion charge underway. Played on an icy Portman Road pitch, Fulham took a 10th minute lead through Cook from a Leggat pass. Despite losing skipper Pickett after 22 minutes, Ipswich fought back and neat inter-play between Crawford and Rees gave Leadbetter the chance to equalise in the 58th minute. They looked to be getting the point they deserved until Haynes struck. Bristol Rovers fell to a first half Cook goal the following week at the Cottage, a more convincing win than the scoreline suggested. For the first time in 14 months, Fulham went into a game without Macedo in goal. He was injured in the Cup tie at Birmingham, ending a run of 59 successive matches and giving a chance to his brave but eccentric deputy, Ken Hewkins. A 2-0 defeat at Derby put the push on hold,

Teenager Alan Mullery made a sensational debut in February 1959.

but only for a week when Orient were at the Cottage and Mullery made his debut. Strengthened by the re-signing of centre-forward Johnston from Blackburn, Orient were simply blown away by an effervescent Fulham who were two up (Leggat and Doherty) in 10 minutes. Then Haynes took over, and got another splendid hat-trick. The fact that Baily and Andrews scored for the visitors was not really important. Fulham were well and truly on their way, back in second place, two points clear of Liverpool (but four adrift of Wednesday) and never again that season to relinquish a promotion place.

Despite being weakened by a flu outbreak at the Cottage, Fulham managed a win at Scunthorpe, thanks to Haynes' last minute goal, cleverly set up by Doherty. A deflection by Lampe in the first half had given the home side a lead they held until Leggat was fouled in the box and Langley buried the spot kick. The win showed the Cottagers were prepared to fight to the end even when their backs were against the wall. A 25th minute drive from just inside the box by Leggat was enough to overcome Bristol City at the Cottage. It was a deserved win in an entertaining game but the Fulham forwards struggled to convert possession into goals.

Skipper Johnny Haynes who led by example.

Facing Liverpool in front of 43,926 at Anfield was a high hurdle that Fulham had to clear. They had to avoid defeat by their most serious rival for the second promotion place, which they just about managed. The two half-back lines were totally dominant and chances few and far between. The best fell early on to the Reds' Arnell but he missed and a goalless draw was more valuable to Fulham than Liverpool. Middlesbrough, Clough and Taylor included, succumbed at the Cottage despite leading 2-1. But, on the hour, Haynes switched wingers Leggat and Barton and it changed the game. In the 75th minute, Fulham were back on terms, Leggat the provider and the Maestro the scorer. A minute later, Barton beat goalkeeper Taylor to Hill's cross and scored the winner.

New signing Graham Leggat broke a club record scoring in his first few weeks.

The rest of the March programme, which was likely to be decisive, involved three games against teams from Sheffield plus a home match with Grimsby. A visit to Bramall Lane was utterly pointless. A below-par performance got what it deserved – nothing. Only Macedo's heroics kept the score down to 2-0, a 20-yard Hamilton drive in the first half and a Shaw penalty in the second.

Easter began with what was the Match of the Season, the visit of leaders Sheffield Wednesday. Played at 11.15 on Good Friday morning, the game attracted a crowd of 39,377. Wednesday, on 48 points from 32 games, led Fulham, 47 points from 34 games, by the narrowest of margins. With 15 minutes to go, there was not much between the teams. Leggat scored for Fulham after just six minutes but Wilkinson equalised with a header on 20. When Staniforth handled Cook's goal-bound shot on the line, it gave Langley the chance to restore Fulham's lead from the spot. But again Wednesday came back, and a hook shot by Shiner levelled the scores two minutes after the change of ends. Just after the hour, Cook put the Cottagers ahead for the third time and there it stood at 3-2 until the 75th minute.

For much of the season, Hill had struggled in front of goal. After scoring 22 the previous season, all he had managed were two goals in the FA Cup in 29 appearances. There were even suggestions of a bust-up between him and chairman Trinder before the game and speculation about him being dropped for the visit of Wednesday. But Jezzard kept faith with his controversial bearded inside-forward and was well rewarded. From left footed Chamberlain's corner on the right, Hill soared to head home a vital fourth. Just four minutes later, he rounded off a Haynes-Cook move with his head and then two minutes from time completed his hat-trick – with his head. A remarkable game topped off by a remarkable individual performance which resulted in a 6-2 win for Fulham, two points that put them on top of the table with seven games to go.

The next day, Grimsby were beaten without Fulham getting into top gear. A rejuvenated Hill made the first goal for Haynes in the 18th minute and Langley set up Leggat for the second on the hour. In the final 10 minutes, Fulham were awarded two penalties, the first when Leggat was fouled from which Langley scored, and the second when Donovan handled, which goalkeeper Barnett saved. The Cottagers did enough for the two points and probably had their minds on the visit to Hillsborough on Easter Monday.

In another epic encounter, Wednesday and Fulham shared four goals and the two points. Cook gave Fulham a 17th minute lead, which Shiner equalised 12 minutes later after Langley got caught in possession. It was just 13 seconds into the re-start that Fantham scored from 18 yards after a goalmouth scramble. Wednesday might have increased their lead but for two stunning saves by Macedo. Then, with only 14 minutes to go, Cook saved the day. A Bentley clearance found Leggat on the right. He ran and slipped the ball past the advancing 'keeper McLaren but Staniforth cleared. His clearance, however, went to Cook who fired in a rocket shot.

With five points from a possible six over Easter, Fulham were ideally placed. They topped the table on 52 points, Wednesday were second on 51 and Liverpool third with 46. The Cottagers had, however, played two more games than both of their rivals. Promotion was theirs to lose and it took three more games to clinch it.

The first of these was a trip to Cardiff where Fulham claimed the three points relatively easily despite conceding a sloppy goal after just 25 seconds. Langley's clearance cannoned off Tapscott to Walsh, who scored easily. Although the visitors then had the better of the exchanges, there was no more scoring until the 74th minute when Hill fed Leggat and the Scot fired in through a crowded penalty area. Then, with just eight minutes left, a mix-up in the Cardiff area let Haynes through. His shot went in off two defenders and barely trickled over the line. It was enough. Even without Haynes and Leggat, Fulham overcame Huddersfield at the Cottage. With Barton and Doherty again deputising, they won a strangely low-key game thanks to Cook's headed goal from Chamberlain's cross two minutes before half-time. But it took a wonder save by Macedo with his feet to deny McHale in the last minute. A defeat that day for Liverpool meant a win for Fulham at bottom-of-the-table Barnsley the following week would seal one of the top two places.

For the first 20 minutes at Oakwell it was difficult to tell which of the teams was challenging for promotion and which was threatened with relegation. Barnsley did most of the early attacking without reward and then Fulham broke away and scored, a Leggat cross giving Hill the easiest of chances. In the first minute of the second half, however, McCann scored for the Tykes. Hill presented Cook with the easiest of chances to give Fulham the edge on the hour, but Barnsley would not give up. Following a Butler free-kick, Beaumont hooked in a second equaliser. But then the key moment. In the 71st minute, defender Bartlett, trying to turn a Chamberlain cross away for a corner, sent the ball crashing into his own net. To rub salt into Barnsley's wounds, Leggat got a fourth minutes from the end after a Chamberlain shot came back off the post.

So, 10 years after their first promotion to the top flight, the Cottagers secured the second. They lost in midweek at Charlton, to a goal by former Fulham player Summers. A Hill header had equalised Lawrie's earlier effort but there was no coming back from Summers delightful strike seven minutes from time. The final match was a home game, against Rotherham and it gave the supporters the chance to celebrate. On a very wet April afternoon, almost 18,000 turned up for a game with nothing at stake. A relaxed Fulham were two up at half-time, both scored by Haynes, after five and 26 minutes, both well-taken after neat passing movements. With 11 minutes to go, Rotherham's left-back Morgan handled in the area and instinctively, Haynes picked up the ball and called up regular penalty taker Langley to take the kick. His teammates would have none of it yet the Maestro had to be persuaded to take it himself to complete his hat-trick. The season was over. Promotion had already been secured and the match was won, yet Haynes was still putting the team first. He was the consummate professional. He scored, completed his fourth hat-trick of the season, Hill added another goal two minutes later and the season ended with a 4-0 win.

Reflections

In the end, Fulham finished in second place with 60 points, three more than it took to win the title 10 years earlier. They had a seven-point margin over Sheffield United in third. This was at the time the most successful season in the club's history, with most wins (27), most home wins (18) and fewest defeats (9). For manager Jezzard, a playing member of the 1948-49 side, it was a very satisfying debut. He could look at the performances of established internationals like Haynes, Langley and Leggat, and the emerging talent of youngsters such as Macedo, Cohen and Mullery, and feel he had some quality material to work with at a higher level. And there were probably a few more miles left in veterans like Lowe, Bentley and Hill.

Although 23 players were used during the campaign, there were 11 who played in at least half the matches. The preferred first team changed very little during the season. In fact, of the line-up that started against Stoke in August (Macedo, Cohen, Langley, Bentley, Stapleton, Lowe, Leggat, Hill, Cook, Haynes, Chamberlain) 10 played in the final match against Rotherham in April. The only change was Bentley replacing Stapleton at centre-half and Mullery coming in at right-half. The expecta-

tions at the start of the season had been fulfilled and the disappointment of 12 months earlier was overcome. But a much bigger challenge awaited them.

The programme for the Match of the Season, the Good Friday meeting with Sheffield Wednesday.

Summary Statistics

End	Played	Points	Position
September	10	19	1st
October	14	23	2nd
November	19	30	1st
December	24	34	2nd
January	27	38	2nd
February	31	44	2nd
March	37	52	1st
April	42	60	2nd
Final	**42**	**60**	**2nd**

	H	A	Total
P	21	21	**42**
W	18	9	**27**
D	1	5	**6**
L	2	7	**9**
F	65	31	**96**
A	26	35	**61**
Pts	37	23	**60**

0 points v	*1 point v*	*2 points v*	*3 points v*	*4 points v*
	Liverpool	Brighton & HA	Bristol C	Barnsley
		Charlton A	Bristol R	Cardiff C
		Derby C	Grimsby T	Ipswich T
		Huddersfield T	Scunthorpe U	Leyton O
		Rotherham U	Sheffield W	Lincoln C
		Sheffield U		Middlesbrough
		Stoke C		Sunderland
		Swansea T		
0 points	**1 point**	**16 points**	**15 points**	**28 points**

Appearances

Goalkeeper:	Macedo 37, Hewkins 5
Right-back:	Cohen 41, Lawler 1
Left-back:	Langley 39, Lawler 2, Collins 1
Right-half:	Mullery 14, Lowe 12, Bentley 11, Lawler 5
Centre-half:	Bentley 24, Stapleton 16, Lampe 2
Left-half:	Lawler 21, Lowe 20, Edwards 1
Outside-right:	Leggat 29, Barton 7, Key 3, Cook 2, Stevens 1
Inside-right:	Hill 32, Barton 8, Doherty 1, O'Connell 1
Centre-forward:	Cook 39, Doherty 3
Inside-left:	Haynes 34, Doherty 7, Stevens 1
Outside-left:	Chamberlain 24, Leggat 7, Johnson 6, Key 3, Stevens 1, Langley 1

The Promotion Squad: 1958-59

Tony Macedo: In his first full season, the 20-year-old Macedo established himself as one of the brightest goalkeeping prospects in the country. The Gibraltar-born son of a Spanish international goalkeeper, Macedo had all the characteristics of the best continental goalkeepers. He was brave, flamboyant and acrobatic but prone to the occasional lapse. He stayed at the Cottage until 1968, playing 391 League and Cup games and, after a short spell with Colchester, went to South Africa. Regarded by many as Fulham's best-ever 'keeper, he returned to the Cottage in 2011 for the first time in over 40 years.

George Cohen: Like Macedo, a product of Fulham's juniors who was in his first full season in the League team, Cohen was to go on to play 37 times for England, including the 1966 World Cup Final. He is still number four on Fulham's all-time appearances list but his total of 459 games would have been higher but for the injury that effectively ended his career in 1967 when he was still only 28. An outstanding player and one of Fulham's favourite sons, Cohen can still be seen at the Cottage every home match.

Jimmy Langley: A natural crowd pleaser with his bow legs, crew cut hair, bicycle kicks and exuberant attitude, Langley was signed from Brighton for just £12,000 in 1957. He won three England caps the previous season and was one of the best left-backs in the country. A Fulham player for 356 games until he was controversially sold by

Vic Buckingham in 1965, he went on to further honours with QPR and was involved in non-League football until 1985. He worked as a steward at the Hillingdon British Legion and died aged 77 in 2007.

Alan Mullery: Unquestionably one of the best players ever to emerge from Fulham's juniors, Mullery made the breakthrough in February 1959, the start of a career that encompassed 785 League and Cup appearances for Fulham and Spurs, 35 England caps, two FA Cup Finals, League Cup and European Cup Winners Cup winners' medals and an MBE. He was also featured on *This Is Your Life*. A subsequent management career took him to Brighton, Charlton, Crystal Palace, QPR and Barnet. Now in his 70s, Mullers works as television pundit and is a matchday regular at Craven Cottage.

Roy Bentley: Already in his 30s when he signed for Fulham in September 1956, Bentley was Chelsea's record goalscorer and had captained their 1955 Championship winning side. He held a dozen England caps and had also played for Bristol City and Newcastle. Moving him from the forward line to half-back was a masterstroke by Dug Livingstone. It added years to Bentley's career and gave Fulham (and later QPR) the benefit of a very classy and intelligent footballer. He went into management with Reading and Swansea in the late 1960s and today, in his 80s, lives in retirement in the Reading area.

Eddie Lowe: Signed from Aston Villa in 1950, Lowe was one of three survivors of Fulham's first spell in the top flight. He had played 117 times for Villa and three for England and went on to make 511 appearances for Fulham, second only to Johnny Haynes. A left-sided defender who converted to centre-half late in his career, he was highly rated by his teammates. Not the most mobile of players, Lowe's skills were tackling, passing and positional play. He left Fulham in 1963, tried management with Notts County but left after two years to pursue a business career. He settled in Nottingham and bowls became a passion in retirement. He died in 2009, aged 83.

Robin Lawler: The fair-haired Irish defender and club snooker champion was one of three players Frank Osborne signed from the bankrupt Belfast Celtic club in 1949. He was a regular throughout the 1950s but nearing the end of his playing career by 1959. An early exponent of the long throw, Lawler played eight times for the Republic of Ireland. He worked for Deans Binds for 21 years until ill-health forced his retirement and he died at the age of 73 in 1998.

Graham Leggat: Among Fulham's best-ever transfer signings, Leggat was an immediate success when he joined from Aberdeen in 1958, contributing 21 goals to the promotion side. A winger initially who later switched to centre-forward, he set all sorts of club scoring records. His total of 134 goals in 280 outings included a century in the top flight, the only Fulham player to reach this milestone. His three goals in three minutes against Ipswich in 1963 remains the fastest-ever top-flight hat-trick. The winner of 18 caps and Scottish League and Cup medals with Aberdeen, Leggat was also a fine golfer. Another victim of the Buckingham purge at Fulham, he had short spells with Birmingham and Rotherham before going to Canada and carving out a successful career as a sports analyst on television. He still lives in Canada in retirement.

Jimmy Hill: Probably one of the best-known personalities in British football, Hill was a player, trade union leader, manager, TV analyst, director and chairman at a variety of places including Brentford, Fulham, Coventry, the PFA, the BBC, ITV, Charlton, Fulham again and Sky Television. He spent 10 years at the Cottage as a player and in his 297 appearances in several positions was noted more for his energy and commitment than his skill. Always outspoken and never a man to shun controversy, Hill was somebody about whom few people were neutral. Now well into his 80s and in poor health, he lives in retirement in Sussex.

Maurice Cook: A journeyman centre-forward who was signed from Watford by Livingstone in 1958, Cook fitted in perfectly at Fulham. He scored 97 goals in 248 appearances spread over eight seasons at the Cottage. Ungainly and a bit slow, he was hard and fearless and an excellent target man who never stopped working for the team. Yet another Buckingham victim, he had a season at Reading before dropping into non-League. Cook had a difficult personal life and struggled at times with life after football. He died aged 75 in 2006, on the eve of a Fulham v Watford match.

Johnny Haynes: Without doubt, Fulham's finest-ever player who was also one of the outstanding British footballers of the post-war generation. His 658 appearances and 158 goals for Fulham were both club records, and he was only the fourth player to win 50 caps for England, captaining his country on 22 occasions. Loyal, gifted and inspirational, Haynes was a one-club man who only ever wanted to play football, not manage, coach or talk about it. He left the Cottage in 1970, finished his career in South Africa and then settled in Edinburgh, where he died in 2005, the day after his 71st birthday.

Tosh Chamberlain: In a team of real talent, Chamberlain was an outstanding personality whose love of playing and affection for the club helped define the image of Fulham in the 1950s. A school friend of Haynes (the two remained close until the Maestro's death), he was a Fulham amateur in 1949, a professional in 1951, made his debut (scoring with his first touch of the ball) in 1954 and a regular the following season. He scored 64 goals in his 204 appearances, many with ferocious left foot drives. He left Fulham in 1965 for non-League football and is still today, in his 70s, an occasional and welcome visitor to the Cottage.

1958-59

League Division Two   Manager : Bedford Jezzard

No		Date	V	Opponents	R	H-T	F-T	Scorers	Attend
1	A	23	H	Stoke C	W	4-0	6-1	Cook 3, Haynes, Leggat, Chamberlain	31,846
2		27	A	Sunderland	W	2-0	2-1	Leggat, Chamberlain	37,772
3		30	A	Swansea T	W	1-0	2-1	Haynes, Leggat	25,215
4	S	3	H	Sunderland	W	1-2	6-2	Haynes 3, Chamberlain, Leggat, Langley	26,393
5		6	H	Ipswich T	W	2-2	3-2	Haynes, Cook, Leggat	33,714
6		10	A	Lincoln C	W	0-2	4-2	Leggat 2, Chamberlain, Haynes	13,092
7		13	A	Bristol R	D	0-0	0-0		30,008
8		17	H	Lincoln C	W	2-0	4-2	Haynes 4	20,591
9		20	H	Derby C	W	1-2	4-2	Haynes 2, Langley, Cook	31,756
10		27	A	Leyton O	W	1-0	2-0	Chamberlain, Cook	24,431
11	O	4	H	Scunthorpe U	D	0-0	1-1	Leggat	24,569
12		11	A	Grimsby T	D	0-2	2-2	Langley, Chamberlain	16,778
13		18	H	Liverpool	L	0-0	0-1		43,926
14		25	A	Middlesbrough	W	3-1	3-2	Leggat 3	31,973
15	N	1	H	Sheffield U	W	1-1	4-2	Key, Haynes, Cook, Leggat	32,054
16		8	A	Bristol C	D	1-1	1-1	Haynes	32,378
17		15	H	Cardiff C	W	1-0	2-1	Cook, Chamberlain	24,078
18		22	A	Huddersfield T	L	0-0	1-2	Key	19,778
19		29	H	Barnsley	W	1-0	5-2	Leggat 2, Doherty, Cook, (Houghton og)	18,523
20	D	6	A	Rotherham U	L	0-2	0-4		7,430
21		13	H	Charlton A	W	0-0	2-1	Johnson 2	18,549
22		20	A	Stoke C	L	0-3	1-4	Barton	18,473
23		26	H	Brighton & HA	W	1-0	3-1	Johnson, Cohen, Langley	28,639
24		27	A	Brighton & HA	L	0-1	0-3		36,342
25	J	3	H	Swansea T	L	0-1	1-2	Cook	27,613
26		17	A	Ipswich T	W	1-0	2-1	Cook, Haynes	15,960
27		31	H	Bristol R	W	1-0	1-0	Cook	23,820
28	F	7	A	Derby C	L	0-2	0-2		21,678
29		14	H	Leyton O	W	3-1	5-2	Leggat, Doherty, Haynes 3	20,478
30		21	A	Scunthorpe U	W	0-1	2-1	Langley (pen), Haynes	10,086
31		28	H	Bristol C	W	1-0	1-0	Leggat	26,891
32	M	7	A	Liverpool	D	0-0	0-0		43,926
33		14	H	Middlesbrough	W	1-0	3-2	Leggat, Haynes, Barton	26,800
34		21	A	Sheffield U	L	0-1	0-2		17,828
35		27	H	Sheffield W	W	2-1	6-2	Leggat, Langley (pen), Cook, Hill 3	39,377
36		28	H	Grimsby T	W	1-0	3-0	Haynes, Leggat, Langley (pen)	25,059
37		30	A	Sheffield W	D	1-1	2-2	Cook 2	32,055
38	A	4	A	Cardiff C	W	0-1	2-1	Leggat, Haynes	23,217
39		11	H	Huddersfield T	W	1-0	1-0	Cook	20,907
40		18	A	Barnsley	W	1-0	4-2	Hill, Cook, Leggat, (Bartlett og)	8,068
41		23	A	Charlton A	L	0-1	1-2	Hill	22,129
42		25	H	Rotherham U	W	2-0	4-0	Haynes 3 (1 pen), Hill	17,861

Apps
Goals

				FA CUP					
3	J	10	H	Peterborough U	D	0-0	0-0		31,908
R		24	A	Peterborough U	W	1-0	1-0	Johnson	21,400
4		28	A	Birmingham C	D	1-0	1-1	Hill	42,677
R	F	4	H	Birmingham C	L	2-2	2-3	Leggat, Hill	27,521

Macedo	Cohen	Langley	Bentley	Stapleton	Lowe	Leggat	Hill	Cook	Haynes	Chamberlain	Lawler	Stevens	Doherty	Key	Barton	Lampe	Johnson	O'Connell	Hewkins	Collins	Mullery	Edwards	#
1	2	3	4	5	6	7	8	9	10	11													1
1	2	3	4	5	6	7	8	9	10	11													2
1	2	3	4	5	6	7	8	9	10	11													3
1	2	3		5	6	7	8	9	10	11	4												4
1	2	3		5	6	7	8	9	10	11	4												5
1	2	3		5	6	7	8	9	10	11	4												6
1	2	3	4	5	6	7	8	9	10	11													7
1	2	3	4	5	6	7	8	9	10	11													8
1	2	3	4	5		7	8	9	10	11	6												9
1	2	3	4	5			8	9	10	11	6	7											10
1	2	3	4	5		7	8	9		11	6	10											11
1	2	3	4	5		7		9	10	11	6		8										12
1	2	3	4	5				9	10		6	11		7	8								13
1	2	3	5		4	7		9	10		6		11		8								14
1	2	3	5		6	7		9	10		4		11		8								15
1	2	3	5		6	11	8	9	10		4				7								16
1	2	3			4	7	8	9		11	6		10				5						17
1	2	3	5		4		8	9		11	6		10	7									18
1	2	3	5		4	7	8	9		11	6		10										19
1	2	3		5	4	7	8	9		11	6		10										20
1	2	3	5		4		8	9			6		10		7		11						21
1	2	3	5		4			9			6		10		7		11	8					22
1	2	3	5		4	7		9	10		6				8		11						23
1	2	3	5		4	7		9	10		6				8		11						24
1	2	3	5		4	7	8	9	10		6						11						25
1	2	3		5	4	7	8	9	10		6						11						26
	2		4	5	6	7	8	9	10		3		11						1				27
	2	11	5		4	7		9	10		6				8				1	3			28
	2		5		6	11	8		10		3		9		7				1		4		29
		3				11		7	10		2		9		8		5		1		4	6	30
	2	3	5			11		7	10		6		9		8				1		4		31
1	2	3	5			11	8	9	10		6				7						4		32
1	2	3	5		6	11	8	9	10						7						4		33
1	2	3	5		6	11	8	9	10						7						4		34
1	2	3	5		6	7	8	9	10	11											4		35
1	2	3	5			7	8	9	10	11	6										4		36
1	2	3	5			7	8	9	10	11	6										4		37
1	2	3	5		6	7	8	9	10	11											4		38
1	2	3	5		6		8	9		11			10		7						4		39
1	2	3	5		6	7	8	9	10	11											4		40
1	2	3	5		6	7	8	9	10	11											4		41
1	2	3	5		6	7	8	9	10	11											4		42
37	41	40	35	16	32	36	32	41	34	24	29	3	11	6	15	2	6	1	5	1	14	1	A
-	1	7	-	-	-	21	6	17	26	7	-	-	2	2	2	-	3	-	-	-	-	-	G

Macedo	Cohen	Langley	Bentley	Stapleton	Lowe	Leggat	Hill	Cook	Haynes	Chamberlain	Lawler	Stevens	Doherty	Key	Barton	Lampe	Johnson	O'Connell	Hewkins	Collins	Mullery	Edwards	#
1	2	3	5		4	7	8	9	10		6						11						3
1	2	3	5		4	7	8	9	10		6						11						R
1	2		4	5	6	7	8	9	10		3						11						4
	2		4	5	6	7	8	9	10		3		11							1			R

4.

The Dodgin Turnaround: 1970-71

Background

If Fulham had an 'annus horriblis', then it was 1968. They started the year at the bottom of the (old) First Division (where they had been since the promotion of 1959) and were relegated in May. They finished the year at the bottom of the Second Division and were relegated to the third tier for the first time in 37 years. In that 12 month period, only nine of the 50 League and Cup games were won, and 29 lost, 30 different players were tried by four managers. The first manager was Vic Buckingham who departed unlamented when his contract expired in January. Next was Bobby Robson, whose playing career with Fulham had only ended the previous May. As good a manager as he was to become, this was too big a challenge for a first job. Nevertheless sacking him after just 10 months was pretty shabby treatment. Reluctantly and temporarily, Johnny Haynes held the fort until a permanent successor was found, and he arrived in December.

Bill Dodgin was the son of a former Fulham manager (also called Bill) and had two spells at the Cottage as a player either side of nine years at Highbury. A rather gangling and awkward full-back or centre-half, his career was effectively ended by a broken leg in 1963. He began coaching at Millwall but when he linked up with Alec

Stock at Loftus Road in 1966, the two guided the club to new heights. They won the League Cup at Wembley as a Third Division side and were promoted in successive seasons to the First Division. When Rangers struggled in the top flight, Stock left and Dodgin took over but he departed in November 1968. A month later, he was back at his old club.

It would not have taken Dodgin long to realise that Fulham were a club in free fall. Many on the playing staff were past their best and others were rather demoralised. Off the field, the board had committed to building the riverside stand which was to be a financial millstone for years to come. To stop the rot required more than tinkering at the edges. A fundamental overhaul was required and the new manager was prepared to do it. An early casualty was his original mentor. Johnny Haynes played the last of his 658 Fulham games in January 1970 and Barry Lloyd, a Dodgin signing, was his successor, in midfield and as captain.

There were signs of improvement in 1969-70, but only late in the season. Just two defeats in the last 20 games showed that the Cottagers were adjusting to the demands of the division but it was only enough to take them up to fourth place (only two up and no Play-offs), five points (two for a win) short of second-placed Luton. But a Dodgin style was emerging, one based on attack. Fulham were the division's highest scorers and both Conway and Earle got more than 20 goals. In the 1970 close season, much of the gloom had lifted to be replaced by a cautious optimism.

The promotion squad. Back row, left to right: Bill Dodgin (manager), Robertson, Horne, Dunne, Richardson, Seymour, Webster, Moreline, Roberts, Callaghan, Tranter, George Cohen (youth coach), Terry Medwin (coach). Front row: Matthewson, Pentecost, Conway, Lloyd, Earle, Halom, Barrett, Brown. Seated: Brickell, Graham, Johnson, James, Fraser.

Leading The Way

A key lesson from the previous season was the importance of a good start, and in the early weeks of 1970-71, the Cottagers got off to a flyer. Up to the end of September, they had won seven and lost only one of the first 10 matches and finished the first phase of the campaign a point ahead of Aston Villa at the top of the table. Survivors of the club's First Division days formed nucleus of the side, defenders Fred Callaghan and Stan Brown, wingers Jimmy Conway and Les Barrett and striker Steve Earle. There were also two Robson signings, Reg Matthewson, who arrived in chaotic final months of top-flight football, and Vic Halom, acquired in the early months of Second Division football. Dodgin's contribution was goalkeeper Malcolm Webster from Arsenal, central-defender Jimmy Dunne from Torquay in the close season, and Lloyd, who arrived at the Cottage in the deal that took John Dempsey to Stamford Bridge. The manager also gave a chance to David Moreline, a product of the youth team and who had played a handful of games at the end of the previous season, to establish himself at full-back. These were the players, with just one mid-season addition, who took Fulham back to the Second Division.

Starting as they meant to continue, Fulham went to Oakwell on the opening day of the season and beat a Barnsley side which seemed intent on defending for the whole 90 minutes. A Brown through ball set up the one goal of the game from Barrett after 63 minutes and only goalkeeper Arblaster stood between Fulham and

a more convincing win. A Winstanley header against the bar in the closing minutes was as close as the Tykes came to scoring. The Cottage welcomed back an old favourite for the first home League game of the season. Roy Bentley was manager of Swansea City but his defensively-minded team had no answer to a rampant Fulham attack. Earle led the charge with two goals, and was supported by Halom and Dunne. But it could have been 10 so poor were the visitors. The Swans' first half goal came from Cotton when the score was 2-0. There was something of a setback at Walsall the following week and an indication of the team's defensive frailties. There were

Manager Bill Dodgin.

Dunne scores in the opening game against Swansea.

four goals in a frantic opening 45 minutes. Lloyd equalised the Sadlers' early goal by Taylor, and then Halom made it 2-2 after Woodward put the home side ahead. The deciding goal came from a penalty converted by Taylor in the second half.

Just days later, Dodgin's men showed the Walsall result was an aberration and gave notice of their promotion credentials. Not only did they cruise to a 5-0 win but all five forwards got on the scoresheet. Conway started the rout after four minutes and then Earle added a second before the break (35) and Halom, whose strength and running had contributed to the first two goals, got the third (52). On the hour, Lloyd made it four from 18 yards and then the best of the lot from Barrett with just two minutes to go. He ran 45 yards, beating three defenders before shooting past the bemused goalkeeper, Roberts.

From the remaining six September matches, Fulham took 10 points from a possible 12. There were home victories over Chesterfield (2-0), with an early Earle volley, Brighton (1-0), the previous season's Fourth Division champions, thanks to a goal from future Seagulls manager Lloyd, and Tranmere (2-0), which included a rare Brown goal. Away from home, the Cottagers were just as effective. Rochdale were beaten 2-1 at Spotland, Conway getting the winner from an acute angle from Earle's crossfield pass. But points were dropped. Doncaster, who had future Fulham manager Ian Branfoot at full-back, showed the physical side of the Third Division and left the Cottage with a draw after Conway had given Fulham an early lead. But Fulham sat back and Briggs got an unexpected 69th minute equaliser. There was

also a draw at Preston, a match and opponents that would have a special significance at the season's end. With Webster and Conway both out with injuries, and Ian
Seymour and John Richardson deputising, Fulham were under pressure for much of
the game. They went ahead, however, just after the break through defender Dunne
who headed home from a corner. Preston equalised almost immediately when a
McNab shot was deflected past a helpless Seymour. Manager Dodgin said he was
pleased with the point.

There was no let-up in October and the team went from strength to strength.
Only one of the six games was lost and after more than a third of the fixtures were

Lloyd has just scored the winner against Brighton in September.

Barrett on the mark against Bradford City in September.

Lloyd scores the second in a 2-0 win over Chesterfield in September.

completed, Fulham led the table on 23 points, followed by Villa on 22 and Bristol Rovers on 21. Come May, however, Dodgin would probably look back at a couple of home draws in October that were points dropped rather than won and which would prove to be expensive in the final count. Despite the impressive start, the manager felt he needed to strengthen the squad, and typically went for an attacking player rather than a defender. He spent £6,000 on Birmingham's George Johnston, once of Arsenal, who was to play a crucial part of the promotion challenge.

October began with a home draw against Plymouth with the visitors again demonstrating brawn rather than brain. Conway was on the receiving end of some harsh treatment and had to leave the pitch. Earle gave Fulham the lead at the start of the second half but an Allen header denied them both points. Without Brown and Conway, the Cottagers travelled to Shrewsbury and emerged with a 1-0 win, courtesy of Barrett's strike from Halom's low cross. Barnsley at home a week later was another disappointment. Dunne was the villain, gifting the visitors a goal with a back pass that left Seymour stranded and presented Lea with an open goal, but Lloyd spared his blushes, heading the equaliser from Earle's cross. A midweek draw at Reading, on the other hand, was definitely a point won. Halom's equaliser gave Fulham a draw they hardly deserved after a lacklustre display but one which kept them top of the table.

The final two games of a wearying month ended in the same scoreline, one a win at home over Halifax the other a defeat at Torquay. Debutant Alan Morton, in for injured Conway, opened the scoring after 17 minutes but then had to go off injured.

A Lloyd header equalises and earns a point against Barnsley in October.

Lloyd and Earle got the other two in a sparkling display. The same could not be said of the trip to Plainmoor. After holding Torquay to 0-0 in the first half, Fulham conceded three in the second before Johnston, making his debut, got a consolation five minutes from time.

Cup Intermission

If there was a reason for the Cottagers losing their edge in October, it was a rare extended run in the League Cup. As well as the six League games they had two in the League Cup which took them to the quarter-finals for only the second time their history. The run started in August with a 1-0 home win over Orient followed by an easy 4-0 disposal of Darlington in round two. Next was a glamour tie, at home to Second Division QPR, which attracted the last 30,000 crowd to the Cottage (31,727). It marked the return of old favourite Rodney Marsh but Fulham were too good on the night and goals by Halom and Barrett took Dodgin's new team to victory over his previous club. Swindon fell at the Cottage in round four to a third-minute Earle strike. Although the visitors had most of the chances, they were wasteful in front of goal and Fulham claimed another higher-division scalp.

But that was as far as it went. In the pouring rain at the Cottage, they missed a great opportunity of going through to the last four, drawing 0-0 with Bristol City, managed by future Fulham boss Alan Dicks. Despite dominating the game, the

Cottagers lost the replay to a penalty, awarded when Brown checked Skirton and converted by Sharpe. An equally obvious penalty for a foul on Barrett in the last minute was denied by referee Jack Taylor.

Days earlier, Fulham had been in action against the other Bristol club, Rovers, for an FA Cup tie, this time at home. The match pitted father Bill, the Rovers manager, against son Bill, and age won out. Fulham went down 2-1 and lost all interest in Cup competitions. From now on, it was just the League.

Stumbling Into The New Year

Most promotion-chasing sides hit a bad patch during the season. How long it lasts and how they respond determines whether they get back on track. Fulham's difficult spell came in the middle third of the season. Between November and the end of January, they won four and lost four of 11 matches and the goals seemed to dry up. By the time Mansfield visited the Cottage at the start of February, Dodgin's team had slipped to fourth, four points behind leaders Villa but with a game in hand. Preston and Bristol Rovers occupied the second and third places. There was no obvious reason for the dip in form. Conway excepted, injuries were not a big factor, although the harder grounds might not have suited Fulham's passing game. But Dodgin kept his nerve, and his faith with his team, and tried to play through the lean spell.

There was no sign of a loss of form or staleness when maximum points were taken from November's first two fixtures. Coming on the back of the Torquay defeat, Fulham looked their old selves in patches at home to Bury and were good value for Lloyd's rather fortunate goal (a clearance hit the Fulham captain and rebounded over the line) in the 33rd minute. But they allowed the Shakers back the game and in the 71st minute White levelled the scores. But, five minutes from time, a brilliant Les Barrett shot secured the two points. At a windy Vale Park on a Monday evening, skipper Lloyd was again on the mark, this time with a diving header in the 24th minute from Halom's cross. On the balance of play, Port Vale were probably worth a share of the spoils and Fulham owed a lot to Dunne and Matthewson and the heart of their defence.

A point at Rotherham is never a bad result but the 1-1 draw showed up some of the Cottagers' frailties. They fell behind after Webster, restored in goal, unluckily conceded an own goal when, under pressure, he pushed a Mullen cross into his own net on 18 minutes. He redeemed himself with a couple of outstanding saves later in the game before Johnston salvaged a point in the 76th minute, after Halom flicked on a Barrett cross.

Results had been better than performances for several weeks but when the League programme was resumed after the Bristol Cup trilogy, results started to reflect performances. And it started with the big one, a home game against Villa in front of 16,021 and the Match of the Day cameras. This was the day the Cottagers surrendered their unbeaten home record and top spot in the table with their worst display of the season. Villa were not much better and the game never really caught fire. The two goals which won it for the visitors both came in the closing stages, from Hamilton (78 minutes) and McMahon three minutes later.

Hopes that this was just a bad day at the office were dispelled when Fulham lost their next two games, narrowly at Mansfield (1-0) and convincingly at Swansea (4-1). There were no excuses from Dodgin for the trouncing at the Vetch. 'The side did not show enough effort,' he admitted, 'and we are out of the top three and sinking fast.' There was then a nine-day break over Christmas when Gillingham were the visitors to the Cottage for what was looking to be a vital game. On a snow bound pitch (Dodgin thought the game should not have been played) and in front of the smallest home crowd of the season (7,904), a nervous Fulham bagged both points when Halom squeezed the ball into the net two minutes before half-time.

In retrospect, this was something of a turning point, although it was still a few weeks before Fulham got back into their early-season form. January was a bit better than two preceding months, only one win but just one defeat as well, with the other two games drawn. The first of the draws came in the opening game of 1971, on a quagmire of a pitch at Wrexham. Dodgin played Earle and Barrett on the wings and the game had barely started before Barrett ran through to score. The Cottagers went in at half-time two goals to the good after Ingle panicked and scored in his own goal. The second half was a different story as the Welsh club copied Fulham's tactics and attacked from the wings. They brought on winger Moir who inspired a comeback. May struck the first with a long shot Webster could not reach because of the mud and a dazzling Moir run set up Kinsey for the equaliser. On a Friday evening at Prenton Park, Fulham destroyed Tranmere with three goals in the first half hour. Barrett was the star. He got the first, a header, after 60 seconds and the third after 32 minutes. In between, a ferocious Halom drive from Barrett's cross had made it 2-0 after only four minutes. At Reading the following week, the Cottagers trailed the home side for a long period once teenager Swain scored in the 13th minute. But, after wasting several easier chances, Earle grabbed an 81st minute equaliser from Callaghan's free-kick.

Poor weather led to the postponement of a vital home game against Bristol Rovers and so Fulham had an extra week's break before an equally important match against the leaders and League Cup finalists, Aston Villa. A huge Villa Park crowd of 33,340 saw the home side complete the double over the Londoners in a bad tempered match played on a mud heap of a pitch. The game was only given the go-ahead an hour before kick-off. An over-vigorous Fulham paid the price when Dunne was adjudged to have fouled Anderson in the 55th minute and the same player scored the only goal of the game from the spot. Fulham protested the decision vigorously, Dunne was booked and Dodgin was outspoken afterwards. But it was in keeping with the game that it should have been decided by a penalty. Although the Cottagers welcomed back Conway, he only lasted 70 before falling victim to another poor tackle.

Getting Back On Track

Expensive as that defeat against Villa appeared, the Cottagers got back on track and with a draw and four straight wins re-asserted their promotion push. Especially significant were two wins in the space of three weeks over fellow challengers Bristol Rovers. Just as autumn's loss of form could not be explained by one single factor, neither could spring's recovery. The return of Conway was a huge plus, as were the softer grounds and promotion rivals having their own wobbles. From fourth at the start of February, Fulham climbed back to second at the end of March, with Preston the new leaders.

A dispiriting goalless draw at home to Mansfield in the wake of the defeat at Villa was followed by a run of four straight wins, three at home, when 11 goals were scored and only two conceded. Almost 19,000 packed into Eastville for the match between third-placed Bristol Rovers and Fulham in fourth, with just a point separating the teams. A point still separated them after 90 minutes, but the teams switched places after a Conway goal gave Fulham a vital win. In windy conditions, Rovers had the better of the first half but, after the break, Fulham took control with their younger forwards putting pressure on the home side's ageing defenders. And it was a blunder by veteran Megson that gave Conway the chance to score his first goal since September to seal the points in the 65th minute.

The 4-1 home win over Port Vale was not as comfortable as it seemed. Barrett scored twice in the first 12 minutes, the first after 75 seconds, but again the Cottagers allowed the opposition back in the game. Midfield and defence lost their way completely and it was only wasteful shooting by Vale that kept their tally down to Green's 26th minute effort. But the second half was a different story. Earle and Barrett were at their most menacing and it was two goals from Earle that finally put the game beyond the visitors' reach. There was another four-goal haul six days later. The home game against Torquay was played on a Friday evening to avoid clashing with the League Cup Final the following day. Skipper Lloyd was the mastermind behind the 4-0 win. He set up Barrett for the opener after 11 minutes and had a hand in Conway's second three minutes before half-time, the Irishman catching the goalkeeper off his line. Any hopes Torquay had of a comeback were extinguished with two more goals in two minutes around the hour mark, through Matthewson (his first goal for Fulham and his first for five years) and Barrett again. Temporarily at least, Fulham went back to the top of the table.

Earle scores one of his two goals in the 4-1 win over Port Vale in February.

The hat-trick of wins was competed days later, on a Tuesday, with the re-arranged home fixture with Bristol Rovers. The 2-1 win gave the Cottagers a two-point lead at the top and severely dented Rovers' promotion hopes, but it was not without controversy. After a goalless first half, Fulham took the lead when Johnston collected a cross from Barrett. His shot was only parried by goalkeeper Sheppard and Earle following up, scored. Rovers' defenders claimed Johnston had pushed defender Prince at the start of the move but referee Tinkler disagreed. Within four minutes it was 2-0, Johnston screwing the ball in from the tightest of angles. In the closing minutes, Prince raced through to score while the Fulham defence appealed for an offside whistle that never came. This was an important result and a valuable double for son over father, ample revenge for the FA Cup defeat.

And so Fulham went into March and the final lap in good spirits and in pole position. But they hit a couple of bumps on the road straight away, in the shape of Halifax and Brighton. On the ground where the Cottagers had scored eight, the previous season they looked good for another win when Conway set up Johnston for a goal after 27 minutes. Conway himself should have made it two but lobbed over the bar when unmarked, a miss the visitors would come to regret. Halifax came into the game in the second half and Wallace equalised from 20 yards in the 72nd minute and Holmes headed the winner five minutes later.

It was no better when Fulham went to the seaside the following Wednesday. Apparently Dodgin had tried to sign the former Chelsea player Bert Murray from Birmingham before the transfer deadline but he chose to go to Brighton instead. On his debut for the Seagulls, Murray set up the opening goal after just three minutes, scored by Peter O'Sullivan, who later played a major role in a later Fulham promotion side. Another pass from Murray gave another new boy, Irvine, the chance to make it 2-0. But the Cottagers fought back, and were level at half-time, through Conway and Johnston. There was an element of luck about Brighton's winner. Urged on by their biggest crowd of the season, 14,413, they surged forward and a shot by Napier cannoned off Matthewson into the net with Webster going the other way.

Despite the two away defeats, the other results were kind to Fulham and they were still in second place, two points adrift of Preston having played one game more. Halifax and Villa, however, were hard on their heels just a point behind. So two 1-0 home wins in the space of four days was just what the Cottagers needed to steady their nerves. Neither of the performances, against Rotherham and Wrexham, set the Thames on fire, but at this stage of the season, it was points that counted. In both games, the winning goal came in the second half, Earle in the 69th minute against Rotherham and Barrett in the 72nd against Wrexham.

Upping The Tempo

The odd arrangement of fixtures continued with two away games following on from two home games, and there was a poor return from the trips to Bury and Chesterfield, no goals scored and just one point. Lowly Bury had a habit of tripping up the promotion chasers and counted Villa, Bristol Rovers and Torquay among their scalps. At Gigg Lane, they added Fulham to their collection. Inspired by former England winger Connelly, they scored once in each half to record a comfortable win. But this was the last low point and from here on in, the Cottagers got into top gear, and stayed there. They went on an eight-match

Johnston gets the opening goal in the crucial win over Bristol Rovers in March.

unbeaten run which clinched promotion but then slipped as the title was within their grasp.

At Chesterfield the following Friday, there was much more fight about Fulham and they went all-out for the win. The home defence stood firm however, and they returned to London with a point from a goalless draw. A 1-0 home win over relegation-threatened Walsall, thanks to Barrett's 50th minute goal, was easier than the scoreline suggested and several good chances went begging. In another midweek encounter, a Good Friday fixture brought forward to Wednesday, Dodgin's men were good value for their 2-0 home win over Rochdale, although they had to wait until the second half to break the deadlock. A neat exchange of passes with Johnston gave Earle the chance to beat the goalkeeper from 15 yards. In the 75th minute, Conway ended any doubts when he scored from a penalty awarded for handball.

This win opened up a five-point gap between Fulham in second place and Villa in third, although the Cottagers had played two games more. Dodgin felt relaxed about the club's position, believing points were more important at this stage of the season. Gillingham away on Easter Saturday made it three wins on the trot. At a ground where Fulham have often struggled, they scored three goals in an eight-minute spell at the start of the second half to sink the Gills without trace. The Big Match cameras were there, along with a crowd of nearly 10,000 to see Barrett, Johnston and Conway wipe out bottom-of-the-table Gillingham's first half lead. It would have been a 100 per cent Easter but for Hinch's late equaliser for Plymouth at Home Park on the

Monday. An excellent Halom goal had given the visitors a half-time lead but with three minutes to go they conceded a goal and a point.

The finishing line was within touching distance when Fulham threw away a point in a goalless draw in the penultimate home game, against Shrewsbury. Going into the match, Fulham and Preston shared top spot on 55 points, with Halifax five points adrift and just one game in hand. An injury to Halom disrupted Fulham's attack against Shrewsbury but they still squandered four clear chances to convert their territorial domination into goals and an extra point. This left the Cottagers three games to play, two away in Yorkshire and the final game at home ironically against Preston for what might prove to be a title decider.

Yorkshire proved to be a happy hunting ground for Dodgin's team. They emerged from two games in the space of four days with maximum points and promotion secured. At Doncaster, Fulham played like champions and turned on the style but only for the first 20 minutes. They could have scored three or four times against a team destined to be relegated. But then they fell away, and Rovers started to dominate possession without seriously threatening to score. But, four minutes from time, Fulham were given a free-kick just inside Rovers half. The ball was played out to Barrett on the left and as a defender moved to tackle, he slipped the ball to Earle who scored. It meant not only two precious points but also that a win at Bradford City the following Wednesday would confirm promotion.

There were only 6,430 at Valley Parade that evening. At full strength and unchanged for the fifth consecutive match, Fulham were again wasteful in front of goal and generous in defence. Earle, Barrett and Conway all missed acceptable chances before the Cottagers' flowing football brought them a 32nd minute lead when Johnston was on hand to fire in a loose ball. Just when it seemed as if they would build on this advantage, they conceded a soft goal on the stroke of half-time, Hall the scorer. Johnston should have got his second straight after the interval but the Cottagers had

 to wait until the 55th minute for skipper Lloyd's clever lob to restore their lead. But again, Fulham let Bradford back in the game. In the 70th minute Corner scored with a header. But the visitors had the last word when Johnston sealed victory and promotion in the 75th minute with a superb header.

The programme for the promotion clincher at Bradford in April.

The Big Anti-Climax

All that was left was a home game against Preston three days later and a draw or a win would mean the divisional title would belong at Craven Cottage. The only team that could stop them was Preston, who not only had to beat Fulham but also win their remaining game against Rotherham at Deepdale the following Tuesday. A huge crowd of 25,774, the biggest for a League game for three years, turned up to see a full-strength Fulham complete the job and get the point they needed. The fact that the BBC *Match Of The Day* cameras were once again there was not an encouraging omen.

Halom goes close in the final, deciding match against Preston in May.

Not for the first time, but in a typically Fulhamish way, the Cottagers contrived to muff their lines. The game was a bit of a bore, with North End seemingly happy to play for the point they needed to ensure promotion. The title seemed for them a secondary priority. And then Heppolette dived to head in from Spavin's corner and the visitors were in front after 26 minutes. It was only when Dodgin substituted Halom for Johnston in 72nd minute that Fulham seemed to come alive and offer any threat to the Preston goal. But it was too late as the chance was gone. 'It was an anti-climax for us,' admitted Dodgin after the game. 'The players saved their worst performance for the biggest occasion and were far too cocky and casual.' Needless to say, Preston won their final game and finished as champions, with a point to spare. Fulham claimed second place four points clear of Halifax and seven better than Villa.

Reflections

It was a shame the season ended on a flat note because it obscured what was a remarkable transformation engineered by manager Bill Dodgin in a little over two years. He had turned a club that was sliding south at a rapid rate into promotion winners and got them back to their traditional base of the second tier of the League. They also reached the last eight of the League Cup. In winning promotion, Fulham won more games than any other side in the division and equalled the club record of 60 points in a season, albeit from 46 matches (rather than 42 as in the earlier promotion years).

As with most promotion winners, Fulham benefited from a settled team. Of the 21 players used, 12 appeared in at least half the games and nine played in 30 or more. For much of the season, the team picked itself. Webster was the first choice in goal and the back four comprised Moreline, Matthewson, Dunne and Callaghan, with Pentecost as cover. In midfield, Brown (who made his 350th appearance during the season and had his testimonial match in the autumn) and skipper Lloyd were regulars but Conway's campaign was badly disrupted by injury, which prompted the signing of Johnston. Up front the bustling Halom was the spearhead but the leading marksmen were Barrett (15 goals) and Earle (13 goals). This was the only time that Barrett topped the scoring list. He was ever-present in 1970-71 and extended his run of consecutive appearances to 100.

For Dodgin this was about as good as it got in his time as Fulham manager. He built a team to win promotion but one which came up short the following season at a higher level. It was only a desperate run at the end of the season that prevented the club dropping straight back down. Unfairly, and to the general condemnation of supporters, chairman Trinder sacked Dodgin in May 1972, and replaced him with the manager's mentor from Loftus Road days, Alec Stock.

Summary Statistics

End	Played	Points	Position
September	10	16	1st
October	16	23	1st
November	20	28	1st
December	23	30	3rd
January	27	34	4th
February	31	41	1st
March	38	48	2nd
April	45	60	1st
Final	**46**	**60**	**2nd**

	H	A	Total
P	23	23	46
W	15	9	24
D	6	6	12
L	2	8	10
F	39	29	68
A	12	29	41
Pts	36	24	60

0 points v	*1 point v*	*2 points v*	*3 points v*	*4 points v*
Aston Villa	Mansfield T	Brighton & HA	Barnsley	Bradford C
	Preston NE	Bury	Chesterfield	Bristol R
		Halifax T	Doncaster R	Gillingham
		Plymouth A	Rotherham U	Port Vale
		Reading	Shrewsbury T	Rochdale
		Swansea C	Wrexham	Tranmere R
		Torquay U		
		Walsall		
0 points	**2 points**	**16 points**	**18 points**	**24 points**

The Promotion Squad: 1970-71

Malcolm Webster: A goalkeeper, signed by Dodgin from Arsenal after a loan spell at Fulham, Webster was an English Youth international. He was first choice in the promotion campaign but lost his place to Peter Mellor the following season. Webster later enjoyed success with Cambridge and was goalkeeping coach at both Norwich and Ipswich.

David Moreline: A Londoner who signed for Fulham as an apprentice in 1967, Moreline established himself in the first team during the promotion run. He made 82 appearances for Fulham and then moved to Reading in June 1974 where he played another 166 games before leaving football to become a postman.

Reg Matthewson: It was in 1962 that Matthewson made his League debut for Sheffield United against Fulham. The Blades lost, but he scored and he went on to play 148 times for his home town club. Bobby Robson signed him for Fulham in February 1968 where he proved a model of defensive consistency over five years and 174 games. He finished his career with Chester and was later a coach at Wrexham and Shrewsbury. He now lives in retirement in Chester.

Jimmy Dunne: After spells at Millwall and Torquay, manager Dodgin paid £15,000 to sign Irishman Dunne for Fulham in the summer of 1970. An eccentric character and practical joker, he proved good defensive value and missed only one game in the promotion season. An Irish international, he held his place until the arrival of Bobby Moore and his subsequent travels took him to South Africa, Australia and Devon. Dunne made 166 appearances for Fulham.

Fred Callaghan: A great Fulham character who is still a Cottage regular on matchdays, Callaghan got into the side in 1964 when Mullery was sold to Spurs. A left-back or left-half, he spent 12 years as a player at the Cottage, and was a great crowd favourite. His 336 appearances were in three divisions of the League and both major Cup competitions. Callaghan later managed Brentford and had a long career in non-League football which he combined with being a London cabbie.

Mike Pentecost: A useful and versatile defender who joined Fulham from non-League football in 1966, Pentecost played 95 times during seven years at Fulham.

His wife was South African and he went to play for Durban City in 1973, and settled there. He died in South Africa, aged 63 in 2011.

Jimmy Conway: When he left Fulham in 1976 for Manchester City, Conway had made 356 appearances for Fulham in three divisions of the League as well as playing in the FA Cup Final. He was just 19 when he signed from Bohemians in 1966 and only months later became a first-team regular. Conway was a very modern footballer, something of a winger, inside-forward and wing-half. Very unlucky with injuries, he won 19 Irish caps. In 1978, he went to the US, and then settled in Oregon but now sadly suffers from a rare form of Alzheimer's.

Stan Brown: A Fulham veteran, Brown made his 350th appearance during the promotion season and had a Testimonial match. He had signed professional for Fulham in 1959, made his debut in 1961 and had played in virtually every position for the club. Ultra reliable, Brown was a model professional who had a season at Colchester before settling in Sussex and getting involved in local football. He is 16th on Fulham's all-time appearances list and is an occasional visitor to the Cottage today.

Barry Lloyd: Signed from Chelsea in 1969 as part of the deal that took John Dempsey to Stamford Bridge, Lloyd had the thankless task of succeeding Haynes in midfield and as captain. He was very effective at the heart of midfield and kept the captaincy until the return of Mullery in 1972. In all, Lloyd spent over seven years at the Cottage, playing in 289 games. He moved on to Hereford and then Brentford before going into management at Yeovil and Brighton.

Les Barrett: Only two players have made more than Barrett's 487 appearances for Fulham, virtually all of which were on the left wing. Just 18 when he made his debut in the First Division, Barrett was top scorer in the promotion season and a natural crowd pleaser. A falling out with the manager led to his departure for Millwall in 1977 and, after a spell playing in America, he enjoyed a long second career in non-League football with Woking, latterly as a sweeper. Before his retirement, Barrett ran a small market garden at Earlsfield and visits the Cottage occasionally today.

Vic Halom: A soccer nomad, Fulham was the third of Halom's eight clubs as a player. He was Bobby Robson's last signing as Cottagers' manager and scored 25 goals in his 82 outings for Fulham. His hard running and aggressive style was a valuable complement to the subtler skills of Earle and Barrett. He resumed his wanderings in September 1971 and his later career included playing for Sunderland in the 1973 Cup Final and standing for the Lib Dems in Sunderland North in the 1992 General Election, where he came third.

Steve Earle: Only the sixth player to score a century of goals for Fulham, Earle was another whose Fulham years, 1963-73, spanned three divisions of the League. As a striker, he relied more on speed and stealth than physical strength and in 1973 stepped up to the top flight again with Leicester for a sizeable fee. Earle went to play in the US in 1978, eventually settling in Oklahoma where he combined working in financial services with coaching youngsters.

George Johnston: The only addition to the squad once the season started, Glasgow-born Johnston was brought in to cover for the injured Conway. He had played for Cardiff, Arsenal and Birmingham before joining Fulham. He started well at the Cottage and scored two of the goals in the 3-2 win at Bradford that clinched promotion. But he struggled the following season and moved to Hereford in August 1972.

League Division Three   Manager : Bill Dodgin

No		Date	V	Opponents	R	H-T	F-T	Scorers	Attend
1	A	15	A	Barnsley	W	0-0	1-0	Barrett	8,805
2		22	H	Swansea C	W	2-1	4-1	Earle 2, Halom, Dunne	10,384
3		29	A	Walsall	L	2-2	2-3	Halom, Lloyd	6,176
4	S	2	H	Bradford C	W	2-0	5-0	Halom, Earle, Lloyd, Conway, Barrett	10,328
5		5	H	Chesterfield	W	1-0	2-0	Earle, Lloyd	13,175
6		12	A	Rochdale	W	1-1	2-1	Barrett, Conway	4,790
7		19	H	Doncaster R	D	1-0	1-1	Conway	13,642
8		23	H	Brighton & HA	W	0-0	1-0	Lloyd	13,856
9		26	A	Preston NE	D	0-0	1-1	Dunne	12,105
10		28	H	Tranmere R	W	2-0	2-0	Halom, Brown	10,968
11	O	3	H	Plymouth A	D	0-0	1-1	Earle	13,334
12		10	A	Shrewsbury T	W	1-0	1-0	Barrett	6,415
13		17	H	Barnsley	D	0-1	1-1	Lloyd	12,952
14		21	A	Reading	D	0-0	1-1	Halom	14,169
15		24	H	Halifax T	W	2-0	3-1	Lloyd, Morton, Earle	10,749
16		31	A	Torquay U	L	0-0	1-3	Johnston	7,598
17	N	7	H	Bury	W	1-0	2-1	Lloyd, Barrett	9,390
18		9	A	Port Vale	W	1-0	1-0	Lloyd	8,292
19		14	A	Rotherham U	D	0-1	1-1	Johnston	9,398
20		28	H	Aston Villa	L	0-0	0-2		16,021
21	D	5	A	Mansfield T	L	0-1	0-1		8,051
22		19	A	Swansea C	L	0-2	1-4	Johnston	10,625
23		28	H	Gillingham	W	1-0	1-0	Halom	7,071
24	J	2	A	Wrexham	D	2-0	2-2	Barrett, (Ingle og)	9,712
25		8	A	Tranmere R	W	3-0	3-0	Barrett 2, Halom	4,619
26		16	H	Reading	D	0-1	1-1	Earle	10,141
27		30	A	Aston Villa	L	0-0	0-1		33,340
28	F	6	H	Mansfield T	D	0-0	0-0		9,370
29		13	A	Bristol R	W	0-0	1-0	Conway	18,875
30		20	H	Port Vale	W	2-1	4-1	Barrett 2, Earle 2	10,389
31		26	H	Torquay U	W	2-0	4-0	Barrett 2, Conway, Matthewson	13,012
32	M	2	H	Bristol R	W	0-0	2-1	Johnston, Earle	15,871
33		6	A	Halifax T	L	1-0	1-2	Johnston	8,019
34		10	A	Brighton & HA	L	2-2	2-3	Conway, Johnston	14,413
35		13	H	Rotherham U	W	0-0	1-0	Earle	9,627
36		17	H	Wrexham	W	0-0	1-0	Barrett	8,856
37		20	A	Bury	L	0-1	0-2		4,121
38		26	A	Chesterfield	D	0-0	0-0		13,370
39	A	3	H	Walsall	W	0-0	1-0	Barrett	8,429
40		7	H	Rochdale	W	0-0	2-0	Earle, Conway (pen)	10,054
41		10	A	Gillingham	W	0-1	3-1	Barrett, Johnston, Conway	9,367
42		12	A	Plymouth A	D	1-0	1-1	Halom	11,712
43		17	H	Shrewsbury T	D	0-0	0-0		12,702
44		24	A	Doncaster R	W	0-0	1-0	Earle	4,399
45		28	A	Bradford C	W	1-1	3-2	Johnston 2, Lloyd	6,430
46	M	1	H	Preston NE	L	0-1	0-1		25,774

Apps
Sub
Goals

				FA CUP					
1	N	21	H	Bristol R	L	0-0	1-2	Johnston	13,921
				LEAGUE CUP					
1	A	19	H	Orient	W	0-0	1-0	Conway	10,975
2	S	9	A	Darlington	W	2-0	4-0	Barrett 2, Halom, Conway (pen)	9,324
3	O	6	H	Queen's Park R	W	1-0	2-0	Barrett, Halom	31,727
4		27	H	Swindon T	W	1-0	1-0	Earle	22,576
5	N	17	H	Bristol C	D	0-0	0-0		16,281
R		24	A	Bristol C	L	0-1	0-1		23,249

Webster	Moreline	Callaghan	Brown	Matthewson	Dunne	Conway	Halom	Earle	Lloyd	Barrett	Seymour	Richardson	Pentecost	Davidson	Horne	Morton	Johnston	Roberts	Mansley	Tranter	
1	2	3	4	5	6	7	8	9	10	11			S								1
1	2	3	4	5	6	7	8	9	10	11										S	2
1	2	3	4	5	6	7	8	9	10	11					S						3
1	2	3	4	5	6	7	8	9	10	11								S			4
1	2	3	4	5	6	7	8	9	10	11		S									5
1	2	3	4	5	6	7	8	9	10	11					S						6
	2	3	4	5	6	7	8	9	10	11	1							S			7
	2	3	4	5	6	7	8	9	10	11	1	S									8
	2	3	7	5	6		8	9	10	11	1	4			S						9
	2	3	4	5	6	7	8	9	10	11	1	S									10
		3	2	5	6	7*	8	9	10	11	1	4	12								11
		3		5	6		8	9	10	11	1	4	2	7	S						12
		3	7*	5	6		8	9	10	11	1	4	2			12					13
		3	7	5	6		8	9	10	11	1	4	2		S						14
1		3	4	12	6		8	9	10	11		5	2				7*				15
1		3	4	S	6		8	9	10	7		5	2				11				16
1	12	3	4	6			8	9	10	11		5*	2				7				17
1	S	3	4	5	6		8	9	10	11			2				7				18
1	8	3	4*	5	6		12	9	10	11			2				7				19
		3	4	5	6		8	9	10	11	1		2		S		7				20
	2	3	4	5	6	8*		9	10	11	1					7	12				21
	2	3*	12		6			9	8	10	1				4		7	5	11		22
1	2	8	4	5	6		9	7	10	11		3			S						23
1	2	8	4	5	6		9	7	10	11		3								S	24
1	2	8	4	5	6		9	7	10	11		3								S	25
1	2	6		5	4		8	9	10	11		12	3				7*				26
1	4	3		5	6	7*	9	10	8	11		12								2	27
1	4	3	5*		6	7	12	9	10	11							8			2	28
1	4	3	2	5	6	7	S	9	10	11							8				29
1	4	3	2	5	6	7		9	10	11		S					8				30
1	4	3	2	5	6	7		9	10	11		S					8				31
1	4	3	2	5	6	7		9	10	11		S					8				32
1	3	4	2	5	6	7		9	10	11					S		8				33
1	4	3	2	5	6	7		9	10	11		S					8				34
1	2	3	7*	5	4		12	9	10	11		6					8				35
1	2	3	4	5	6	7		9	10	11		12					8*				36
1	2	3	4	5	6	7		9	10	11		12					8*				37
1			4	5	6	7	8	9	10	11		S	3							2	38
1		3	4	5	6	7	9		10	11			2		S		8				39
1		3	4	5	6	7	S	9	10	11			2				8				40
1		3		5	6	7	9		10	11		12	2		4		8*				41
1		3		5	6	7	9*		10	11		12	2		4		8				42
1		3		5	6	7	9*		10	11		12	2		4		8				43
1		3		5	6	7	12	9	10	11			2		4		8*				44
1		3		5	6	7	S	9	10	11			2		4		8				45
1		3		5	6	7	12	9	10	11			2		4		8*				46

35	28	45	35	43	45	29	30	42	46	46	11	9	22	1	8	1	25	1	1	3	A
-	1	-	1	1	-	-	5	-	-	-	-	7	1	-	1	-	1	-	-	-	S
-	-	-	1	1	2	8	8	13	9	15	-	-	-	-	-	1	9	-	-	-	G

Webster	Moreline	Callaghan	Brown	Matthewson	Dunne	Conway	Halom	Earle	Lloyd	Barrett	Seymour	Richardson	Pentecost	Davidson	Horne	Morton	Johnston	Roberts	Mansley	Tranter	
		3	4	5	6		8	9	10	11	1		2		S		7				1

Webster	Moreline	Callaghan	Brown	Matthewson	Dunne	Conway	Halom	Earle	Lloyd	Barrett	Seymour	Richardson	Pentecost	Davidson	Horne	Morton	Johnston	Roberts	Mansley	Tranter	
1	2	3	4	5	6	7	8	9	10	11		S									1
1	2	3	4*	5	6	7	8	9	10	11				12							2
		3		5	6		8	9	10	11	1	4	2	S		7					3
1		3	4	S	6		8	9	10	11		5	2				7				4
	7*	3	4	5	6		8	9	10	11	1		2				12				5
		3	4	5	6		8	9	10	11	1		2			7		S			R

5.

Candle in the Wind: 1981-82

Background

Reaching the FA Cup Final in 1975 was expected to provide Fulham with a spring-board for a serious attempt to regain their top-flight status. Rather than a spring-board up, however, the Wembley appearance proved to be the top of a long slide down into near-oblivion over the next 20 years or so. During the most turbulent period in the Cottagers' history, they dropped into the League basement, stared at the real possibility of non-League football, were threatened with a merger with QPR and faced the prospect of being evicted from their traditional home on the banks of the Thames. For the club and its supporters, this was a lost generation. It was only in 1997 that the Cottagers emerged from the darkness and began to claw their way back.

The underlying cause of this decline was financial. The burden of financing the new stand along the riverside had allowed an unscrupulous businessman with his own agenda to take control of the club from a naïve board of directors. There were many twists and turns along the way but the direction of the trend line was unam-biguously downwards. It soon became apparent that hopes of promotion after the excitement of the 1975 Cup run were misplaced. Both the ownership of the club and the management changed shortly afterwards, Ernie Clay replacing Tommy Trinder and Bobby Campbell taking over from Alec Stock. Fulham held their own in the (old) Second Division for a few seasons but then, in 1979-80, they were relegated to the Third Division and the long slide was underway.

Well, almost, because even in the darkest times there are moments of hope and for Fulham these came, quite unexpectedly, during Malcolm Macdonald's all-to-brief spell in charge. Following relegation in 1980, the club made a dreadful start in the Third Division. It was clear that manager Campbell had lost the confidence of the players and supporters, to the extent that he no longer sat in the dugout on matchdays and would not agree to the traditional managerial page to appear in the programme. A run of six straight defeats in the autumn, culminating in a 4-0 home defeat by Oxford, marked the end of the Campbell era.

There was no obvious successor. Temporarily, director Ted Drake and physio Ron Woolnough held the fort until the new man was appointed. And the new man was not so new. Malcolm Macdonald had started his playing career at Fulham in Bobby Robson's time but, under-valued by Bill Dodgin, moved on to become one of the best strikers in the country with Luton, Newcastle and Arsenal. When injury ended his career before he was 30, he returned to the Cottage to become Commercial Director. Chairman Clay was persuaded to give 'Supermac' his first shot at football management, despite his relative youth and inexperience.

It was a surprise choice and not universally popular among the supporters. As a player, Macdonald had an image of being brash, arrogant and outspoken and there was no evidence that he had any tactical knowledge or managerial skills. What he did have, however, was an ambition to succeed and great confidence in his own abilities. He also understood his own limitations. Macdonald's view of his role was quite straightforward. He believed he had to create an environment that made it easy for everyone else to do their job effectively, to remove the fear and uncertainty. To succeed, he needed good people around him and slowly he started to build his team.

In his first few months, he could do little more than steady the ship. The drift down the table was halted and Fulham finished 1980-81 in mid-table. This gave him time to assess the squad and he must have been delighted with his inheritance. The team that went down in May 1980 was quite a good one, but had lost self-belief. Players like goalkeeper Gerry Peyton, defenders Kevin Lock, Tony Gale and Les Strong and striker Gordon Davies were all good enough to play at a much higher level. The last of Campbell's signings, Roger Brown, Ray Lewington and Sean O'Driscoll, were now settled at the club and showing their real worth, while the club's most talented group of youngsters for a generation (which included Jeff Hopkins, Paul Parker, Dean Coney, Jim Stannard and Robert Wilson) were ready to make the breakthrough.

All the ingredients were in place, they just needed to be harnessed and motivated. To help him do this, Macdonald recruited two coaches in the summer of 1981, his old Arsenal playing colleague George Armstrong and an unknown but highly recommended Ray Harford, who was at Colchester. What emerged over the next two seasons was some thrilling football which took Fulham to within a whisker of the (old) First Division, played by a team costing no extra money and which clearly enjoyed itself. It was a special time for the club and its supporters which ended well before it had reached its peak. It really was a candle that flickered brightly and briefly but was extinguished very quickly by the financial gale that was enveloping the club.

The promotion squad. Back row, left to right: Hatter, Peters, Wilson, Clement, Stannard, Peyton, Banton, Coney, O'Driscoll, Lock, Greenaway. Front row: O'Sullivan, Lewington, Gale, George Armstrong (coach), Strong, Malcolm Macdonald (manager), Brown, Beck, Davies.

Slow Out of the Blocks

It was a busy close season at the Cottage. Not only did Macdonald recruit his coaches but he made one important signing, left sided midfield player Peter O'Sullivan. Once of Manchester United, 'Sully' had spent most of his career with Brighton. A Welsh international and now at the veteran stage, he was a free transfer (Macdonald did not spend any money on transfers during his tenure) and his tireless running, outstanding control and accurate distribution added an extra dimension to the team. Going into the first season of three rather than two points for a win, the manager was aware of the challenges the club faced. He believed the Third was the toughest division to win since there were seven new teams each season (three down and four up), a turnover far higher than in any other division and a greater range of styles.

For the opening game at home to Brentford, there was a surprise selection. Gale was left out of the starting line-up and Geoff Banton was preferred alongside Roger Brown at the heart of the defence. The manager also gave a home debut to Hopkins at right-back and had John Beck and Clive Day in midfield, alongside O'Sullivan and Lewington. It started well with Coney and Davies demonstrating their almost telepathic understanding. A flicked header by Coney from a long defensive clearance gave Ivor the chance to slam the ball into the net from outside the penalty area. But then, it all went wrong. A penalty and a Brown own goal gave the Bees a half-time lead they held on to relatively easily in the second half. It was then that Fulham took out an insurance policy against having to pay promotion bonuses. For a £3,000 premium, the club stood collect £50,000 if they won the title and £35,000 if they were promoted. After the Brentford game, the insurance company felt its money was safe.

There was trip to Lincoln next for a match that was to be very significant at the end of the season. Gale was back in for Banton and Wilson replaced Day in midfield. Beck, a future Lincoln manager, gave Fulham a deserved first half lead but they found it increasingly difficult to cope with the Imps long ball game, which made full use of their tall, strong front men. With just 10 minutes remaining, the Cottagers conceded another penalty which was converted. A 1-1 draw meant five points out of six had been dropped.

It was not until the third game that Fulham registered their first win, and that was very unconvincing. It came against Bristol City whose assistant manager was a young Roy Hodgson, a manager later to make a huge impact at the Cottage. The Robins were then a club in disarray, recently relegated from Division One and facing financial meltdown. Yet they managed to take the lead when a free-kick was deflected past Peyton by the defensive wall. It was only in the closing minutes that Davies got an equaliser and then, in the final seconds, Brown headed the winner. This was the first of 12 priceless goals the centre-half scored that season, all from open play, which equalled the club record for a defender.

When the Cottagers went down 3-0 at Chesterfield the following week, they dropped to 19th place in the table, albeit after only four games. All the goals that day came in the last 15 minutes but the real problem was a lack of imagination in midfield and movement up front. It was time for the manager to wield the axe.

The Team Takes Shape

Beating Wimbledon 3-1 at Plough Lane in midweek was a significant result. Coney got off the mark for the season with two goals and Davies added the third. It marked the start of a run of eight wins and four draws in 15 games that took the Cottagers into the top four by year end. This was obviously related to the fact that Macdonald had settled on his best team. After the Chesterfield defeat, Beck was dropped and O'Driscoll came in on the right of midfield and, with Wilson now established alongside Lewington and O'Sullivan, the engine room of the side was in place. Fulham had pace down both flanks and competitive ball winners in the middle who not only set up opportunities for Coney and Davies but got forward into scoring positions themselves.

This same team followed the win at Wimbledon with home victories over Chester and Southend. Both performances were workmanlike rather than spectacular but they showed resilience in the team and the four goals came from four different players. O'Driscoll and Lewington were on the mark in the first half against Chester in an otherwise uneventful game. Southend were tougher opponents in every sense of the word and were well worth their half-time lead. The Cottagers came good in the second half and won thanks to goals from Davies and Wilson. These two games amply illustrated the importance of a midfield that could get forward into scoring positions.

September ended encouragingly in fifth position, with Chesterfield, Swindon and Doncaster the pacesetters. October began discouragingly, however, with two away defeats, at Oxford and Huddersfield. At the Manor Ground, where Macdonald had made his League debut 13 years earlier, his team squandered at hatful of chances before United took advantage of the Cottagers' wastefulness with a goal in each half. At Huddersfield, Fulham had young Peter Scott playing the first of his 308 games for

Fulham in place of the injured Lewington but a defensive slip early in the game on a wet surface allowed Town's striker Robins to score the only goal of the game. The Terriers could even afford to miss a penalty and win.

But then the team seemed to click. From the middle of October through to the end of February they lost just one match and lifted themselves into the promotion frame. The three points for a win system was having a beneficial effect. This long period only covered 18 matches because the weather wiped out much of the December and early January fixture list, which was unfortunate timing because Fulham were then in top gear. Some momentum was probably lost because of the extended break.

The run started with two emphatic home wins. Although the Cottagers had much the better of the game against Newport, the scores were level at 1-1 with five minutes left. Then they got a penalty which the reliable Lewington tucked away. There was still time for Davies to get a third and make the scoreline a better reflection of the play. A midweek game a few days later against Exeter produced the best result of the season. Yet again Davies was on the mark and his two goals, plus a Brown header and a shot by O'Driscoll earned Fulham their seventh home win on the trot. There was another double for the Welsh striker, his third in a week, as Fulham came back from a two-goal deficit at Turf Moor to grab a point against in-form Burnley. Davies had so far scored 11 goals in 15 League and Cup games and was on course for his most prolific season. In the Burnley game, another of the promising youngsters was given a chance. Dale Tempest came in for Dean Coney and made a very impressive debut.

After half an hour or so, it seemed inevitable that Macdonald's team would extend their winning home sequence against Portsmouth but they contrived to throw away numerous very presentable chances. Even though Lewington missed a penalty, Fulham looked odds-on for maximum points until early in the second half, a rare Pompey attack led to a goal by Hemmerman. In the end, the home side were grateful for Wilson's late equaliser and the one point that looked for much of the afternoon as though it would be three. The only defeat in the remainder of 1981 came in the first week of November when bottom-of-the-table Plymouth gave their best performance of the season to beat the Cottagers 3-1 on a Tuesday evening at Home Park. Again, it was a case of what might have been if early chances had been taken but, once Cook had given his side the lead, there was no way back and the result did not flatter Argyle. The Fulham manager thought the players were so dominant in the early stages they could score at will. Consequently, they took it easy and when they went behind, could not raise their game.

Winning at Carlisle was important, not just for the three points but it showed the team could travel well. Davies and Coney gave Fulham a 2-0 half-time lead and even though Pop Robson reduced the arrears, the Cottagers were worthy winners. Macdonald reckoned it was an excellent performance and Robson told him Fulham were the best Third Division side Carlisle had played that season. The Fulham manager accepted that the way his team played meant they were always likely to concede goals but he was confident that they would always be able to score more. The match marked the first anniversary of Macdonald's appointment and his first game was coincidentally against Carlisle. That day his team could only draw, so he felt there had been a clear improvement over the 12 months.

That confidence looked misplaced in the next two home games, both of which were televised, both were drawn and both could and should have been won. Although Walsall were in sixth place, one higher than Fulham, they clearly wanted a draw from their visit to the Cottage. The formation was negative and defensive and, despite the fact they took an early lead, they played with very little attacking intent. Brown rescued a point with yet another superb header. Much of the rest of the game was fought out in midfield and the closest either team came to scoring was in the closing minutes when Lewington scraped the bar after rounding the goalkeeper. The elation of the Walsall players at the final whistle showed how much a point meant to them.

Against Millwall, the match was spoiled by a high wind and for the first time that season, Fulham failed to score at home. But the Lions were effectively organised and worth a point. Their line-up that day included Alan Slough, a member of Fulham's 1975 FA Cup Final team, and a very large Sam Allardyce wearing a very small pair of shorts. It was not only the wind that some felt affected Fulham's style. The pitch was thought not to encourage the team's passing style and much of this was attributable to the introduction of rugby league several months earlier. Chairman Clay thought the income from the popular northern code would appeal to exiles in London not to mention the large Australian contingent in Earls Court and help offset the financial impact of relegation.

A Fun Cup Run

Promotion-chasing clubs usually find the Cup competitions an unwelcome distraction, and in the case of the FA Cup this was certainly true of Fulham in 1981-82. After beating Bristol Rovers at Eastville in round one, they went to Hereford, scene of one of Macdonald's less happy playing experiences in his Newcastle days, in round two. There was no real disappointment when Laidlaw scored the only goal of the game for the Fourth Division side.

But the League Cup was different. Not only did the extended run bring in some much needed revenue but it was a chance for Macdonald to see how well his players coped with higher division opposition. Although Fulham unluckily went out in round four (the last 16), he declared himself well satisfied with the team's performances.

It began with a relatively straightforward win over Fourth Division Bournemouth in round one, 1-0 at Dean Court and 2-0 at the Cottage. Macdonald was impressed by the Cherries, however, and tipped them for promotion. (He got it right – they finished fourth.) Coincidentally, the Fulham team in both legs included Peyton, Brown and Beck, who would all later move to Bournemouth from Fulham, as would O'Driscoll who did not play in those games. The second round was special for Macdonald, two games against his former club, Newcastle, then just one division higher. At St James' Park, where the Supermac legend was born and he was a folk hero, the Cottagers stunned the 20,242 crowd by outplaying the Magpies. Goals by Wilson and Coney to one by Barton gave Fulham a win they thoroughly deserved, marred only by an injury to Lewington. The second leg was one-way traffic and goals by Lewington and Coney eased Fulham into round three.

Another Second Division side, Oldham, were the next opponents at the stage where the ties were just one leg. In a closely fought encounter at Boundary Park, the Cottagers earned a replay thanks to a superb five-man move which started with Peyton and was finished off by Wilson. In the replay, the promotion-chasing Latics were crushed 3-0. Hopkins and Coney scored in the opening minutes and Coney capped a fine personal display with a magnificent header for the third goal in the second half. Back at the Cottage for what proved to be the last time was Bill Taylor, then with Oldham but Fulham's coach in the 1975 Cup run. Sadly, days later, he was taken ill and died at the very young age of 42.

A trip to White Hart Lane was the reward for beating Oldham, the Cottagers first for 14 years. In front of a midweek crowd 30,124, Macdonald's team came so very close to upsetting their top-flight opponents and most of the reports felt they had the balance of the play and the better chances. But a first-half Hazard goal won it for Spurs (who went on to the Final). The manager was effusive in his praise of the team, and of Lewington, Peyton, Coney and Davies, but singled out Gale as Fulham's best player. At White Hart Lane, he showed genuine quality at the back and ranked among the best in the country.

An Unwelcome Winter Break

Rather than the five games scheduled for December and the Christmas/New Year holiday period, only two were possible because of appalling wintry weather. This came at a time when Fulham were playing some terrific football and led to inevitable fixture congestion later in the season. In the space of a fortnight the Cottagers twice travelled to Eastville and twice beat Bristol Rovers 2-1, first in the FA Cup and then, more importantly, in the League. The Cup tie was won by two Coney goals and he, along with Davies, were on the mark two weeks later. Coney's goal was a looping volley from the edge of the box while Davies was a splendid solo effort. Rovers' goal came direct from a free-kick. It was almost a month before the Cottagers could play again and at Swindon they gave a superb performance. The 4-1 winning scoreline was the club's best away win for four years and in all departments they were superior to their hosts, better organised at the back, more inventive in midfield and sharper up front. Davies scored twice in the first 25 minutes, substitute Lock got the third with a tremendous volley and O'Driscoll capped a fine individual display with the fourth goal 15 minutes from time. Had they not relaxed in the last quarter of an hour, Fulham's winning margin could have been much bigger. Instead, they allowed

Davies' remarkable winner against Chesterfield in January.

Swindon to pull one back, which seemed to annoy the manager as much as scoring four had pleased him.

The year ended with Fulham in fourth place and playing better than at any stage during the season. They were three points behind Carlisle, having played the same number of games, with Chesterfield and Walsall in between, and the division's top scorers. The benefits of a settle side were apparent. Remarkably, six players (Peyton, Hopkins, Strong, Brown, Davies and O'Sullivan) had played in all 19 League matches, while four others (Gale, Wilson, Coney and Lewington) had each missed only one game.

It was another three weeks before they played again but none of the edge seemed to be lost in the enforced break. The next three games were all won without conceding a goal and two of the victories were against other promotion rivals. By the end of January, Fulham were top of the table, although injuries were starting to accumulate. On a Wednesday evening at Elm Park, Reading were simply swept away by a performance the home team's manager Maurice Evans described as 'devastating'. The match was settled in the first half hour when Fulham scored through Coney and Gale. A second half Lewington penalty completed the rout. The Cottagers outplayed their hosts in every department, despite having Hopkins missing through injury and Wilson through suspension. The experienced and reliable Lock played in defence and young John Reeves was given his League debut.

Fulham went to Griffin Park days later with Davies as well Hopkins and Wilson missing. Tempest was given another game up front and Fulham were much too good for the Bees. A thoroughly disciplined performance, rounded off by O'Sullivan's only goal for the Cottagers, earned them revenge for the opening day defeat. Sully's was the 11th name on Fulham's scoring list so far in 1981-82. The two top teams in the division, Fulham and Chesterfield, both with 38 points from 21 games, met at the Cottage at the end of January, and the match was settled by one of the most remarkable goals ever seen at the ground. Playing towards the Putney End in the first half, a fit-again Davies chased a long ball from the Fulham defence down the left wing. With no other defenders near, Turner in the Chesterfield goal raced out of his area to clear but the Fulham forward beat him to it, took the ball round him and, from the obliquest of angles (he seemed almost to be by the corner flag), deliberately and accurately slotted the ball into an unguarded net. It was the only goal of the game, a breathtaking goal and one that deserved to win any game.

Nerves Start to Show

Having reached the top of the table at the halfway stage, the Cottagers seemed to get a little nervous. Of the five games played in February, only one was won and in three, they failed to score. Nevertheless, they were unbeaten in the month and in spite of dropping eight points from a possible 15, Macdonald's men remained in second place. To make matters worse, at Southend on a Friday evening, Lewington, so crucial in midfield, injured his knee in an innocuous incident which kept him out for the next 14 games.

Coney scores the fourth against Wimbledon in February.

Interest in the game at Bristol City centred on whether the game would take place at all rather than the result. City, deep in debt, were threatened with extinction but a last minute survival plan took them through until the end of the season. It meant most of their senior players were no longer available and manager Roy Hodgson was forced to field a young and inexperienced team. Naturally, in front of the biggest Ashton Gate crowd of the season, the Robins' raised their game while Fulham were below par and had to settle for a share of the spoils in a 0-0 draw. The Cottagers got back to winning ways in midweek at home to bottom club Wimbledon, but not without a scare. After losing their half-time lead shortly after the re-start, they struggled to find their usual rhythm until a fortunate own goal put them back in front. After that, Wimbledon went to pieces and conceded two more, Fulham finally winning comfortably 4-1.

The three remaining February games were all drawn, and the first two, at Southend and at home to Oxford, were both goalless. At Roots Hall against a Southend side also enjoying a long unbeaten run, the game was more exciting than the scoreline implied, with both teams creating chances. Peyton was outstanding in goal for Fulham and this was a point won not two dropped. At home to Oxford the following week, it was a case of two points dropped as the Cottagers were unable to pierce a very well organised defence. In Davies, Coney and Oxford's Cassels, three of the division's highest scorers were on a display, but the scoreline remained blank after 90 minutes. Another two points were let slip at home to Huddersfield. In the opening half hour, Fulham created and wasted a hatful of chances, and then allowed the visitors to score. After the break, a Coney shot and a Lock penalty gave Fulham the edge but, for only the third time that season, they failed to win a match once they were ahead. In the closing minutes, Stanton picked up a clearance from a corner and fired in from fully 30 yards to make it 2-2. Despite the disappointment, the draw stretched the unbeaten run to 13 games and the Cottagers were still in second place, two points behind Carlisle and on the same number of games.

A spectacular O'Driscoll strike against Carlisle in March.

Because of the winter freeze, Fulham went into March with 16 games still to play and some odd results and inconsistent performances in the six games that month saw them slip from top spot to fourth. Fortunately, the other promotion challengers (Carlisle, Reading, Chesterfield and Lincoln) were just as inconsistent and not too much ground in terms of points was lost. And by the end of the month, there were signs that the Cottagers had played their way out of the lean spell.

March started and ended with victories, away at Newport and, crucially, at home to Carlisle. In the 3-1 win in South Wales, Coney scored with a superb 25-yard shot while some inspired play by Davies set up Wilson for another goal. Brown was again on the mark and Fulham scored from three of the five shots they had on target the whole game. The big central-defender was on target twice more against top-of-the-table Carlisle at the Cottage. The television cameras were there to see Brown, Davies and O'Driscoll all score in the opening 25 minutes to kill the game as a contest. Robson pulled one back in the second half but then Brown got his second.

In between these two wins, Fulham showed their indifferent side, drawing two and losing two. In midweek at Exeter they lost their long unbeaten record to a second half goal by Rogers but only after the usually immaculate Lock missed a penalty. This, it became apparent afterwards, was the fault of skipper Les Strong. When the penalty was awarded, he was standing with the Grecians striker Kellow on the halfway line who casually mentioned that Lock always put the ball to the goalkeepers left. When Strong said no, he usually goes to the right, Kellow made frantic signals to his goalkeeper, who went right and saved it. Burnley were emerging as promotion contenders and were pleased to leave the Cottage with a point. A Davies goal was cancelled out by Young before half-time and for all their possession, they could not break down a tough defence that was not slow to use physical strength against Fulham's finesse.

A midweek home defeat by Plymouth (the first home defeat since the opening day of the season) followed days later, which was a very bad day at the office. The only positive note was Tempest's first goal for the club in a bad 3-1 defeat. Argyle were the only club against which Fulham failed to take a single point that season. A possible mitigating factor was that the team was well below full strength. Coney, Gale and Lewington were all absent, in effect the spine of the side. There was, however, a hint that the tide was turning at Fratton Park four days later. Fulham earned a point with a dogged performance and this time, Lock was on the mark from the penalty spot for a second half equaliser. Then came Carlisle, four goals and three points, and a sense of self-belief was coming back.

A Photo Finish

April was almost as good for Fulham as March had been disappointing. They won four and drew one of the seven matches and went into the final month in second place, four points adrift of Carlisle and on the same number of games but two points clear of Lincoln and who had played a game more. As the teams rounded the final bend, this was not a bad place to be. With the weather improving, the playing surfaces were more suited to the Cottagers' style and with only minor injuries affecting the squad, team selection was easy for the manager.

A point at Walsall was hard earned. It was a game the Cottagers were expected to win since the Saddlers had to field a depleted team but, as so often, the youngsters raised their game and made life difficult for their opponents. O'Driscoll got the all-important equaliser but Fulham owed their point to a brilliant display by goalkeeper Peyton. At home to Doncaster in midweek, Rovers were crude and physical but Fulham refused to be provoked and cantered to an emphatic 3-1 victory. Although there was a temporary setback at Gillingham in front of the television cameras, Macdonald was not too downhearted. He felt both sides were committed to winning the game but that his team waited until they were 2-0 up before playing their best football.

O'Discoll's wonderful finish against Bristol Rovers in April.

Then, in a critical seven-day spell, Fulham won three games on trot, scoring nine goals, to haul themselves right back into the frame. Brown's power in the air was the key factor at home to Swindon. He got both goals in a 2-0 win on a Tuesday evening. He was on the mark again on the Saturday against Bristol Rovers at the Cottage, as were Lock and Davies. But the pick of the goals was the fourth and last by O'Driscoll whose spectacular finish rounded off an intricate passing move. The manager felt that the 3-1 away win at Preston in midweek was in many ways the best performance of the season. The home team needed the points to avoid relegation and, with Stannard in goal for the injured Peyton, the Cottagers came back from behind to win 3-1, through Davies (2) and Lock. There was a setback on a Sunday at the Den. Lewington was fit again but Peyton was still missing, and Millwall stormed into a three-goal lead before Fulham really got going. They pulled a couple back through Brown and O'Driscoll but then the Lions got a fourth. A Stevens own goal reduced the arrears but the Cottagers finished on the wrong end of a 4-3 scoreline.

As the final month got underway, it seemed that the three promotion places were between Carlisle, Lincoln, Oxford, Burnley and Fulham, with no one side making a late surge. It was going to be a test of nerve and stamina which would probably go to the very last game. All the second-placed Cottagers could do was to focus on their own performances and not worry about anyone else. Their fate was in their own hands. In what had been an unpredictable season, it was dangerous to make predictions, but with four of the last six games at home, Macdonald fancied his side's chances.

Reading proved a bigger-than-expected obstacle. Davies had to go off with an ankle injury midway through the first half and yet again Fulham conceded a sloppy goal shortly before half-time. Although Wilson levelled the scores the visitors took the lead through Beavon's long-range effort. With only seconds remaining, however, Lewington retrieved the situation when he forced the ball home from close range. Only 1,174 people bothered to turn up for Fulham's midweek trip to Chester and they saw Coney and Tempest, deputising for the injured Davies, steer the Cottagers

Wilson's goal at home to Reading in May.

Tempest gets the match-clinching second goal at Chester in May.

to an efficient win. They came a cropper, however, in another very physical encounter at Doncaster. Rovers had little interest in playing football. Their crude tactics went unpunished but were rewarded with a 2-1 win. With the visit of Gillingham in midweek for a re-arranged fixture, the nerves on the terraces and the pitch were clearly very raw. Still missing their talisman Davies, Fulham had to settle for a 0-0 draw and with all the top teams having just two games to play, there were still four contenders for three places

Another Davies special, this time against Preston in the penultimate game.

Carlisle	77 points
Burnley	76 points
Fulham	74 points
Lincoln	73 points

On the final Saturday of the season, Fulham, again in front of the cameras, turned in as good a home performance as they had all season. With Davies restored up front, they took a two-goal lead in the first 10 minutes against Preston through Davies and Coney. After the interval, Davies added a third to settle the issue, but not

A classic photograph of a classic header, Brown's decisive goal in the final game against Lincoln.

the promotion battle. Although Carlisle had lost, Burnley and Lincoln both won, and thus the congestion at the top was even greater.

So, it call came down to the very last game of Fulham's 55-match season, and, as luck would have it, it was against Lincoln, a game originally scheduled for 9 January but postponed because of the weather. That same Tuesday evening, Burnley were at home to Chesterfield but Carlisle did not play Chester until the next day. The Cottagers knew, however, that a win or a draw would guarantee promotion while nothing less than win would give them any chance of the title. The excitement the game generated was remarkable. Over 20,000 packed into the Cottage on a warm spring evening and were rewarded with 90 minutes of high drama.

Almost immediately, skipper Strong, who was carrying an injury, hobbled off and reserve striker Tempest went to left-back. Lincoln needing the win for promotion had much the better of a tense first half with Cunningham up front proving a real handful. Fulham's Brown played on despite a gash above his eye following a clash of heads and it was he who broke the deadlock in the 58th minute. When Lincoln's Thompson fouled Coney, referee Read had no option but to send him off for a second bookable offence. From the resulting free-kick, Gale floated over an inviting ball for Brown to power his 12th and most important goal of the season. Lincoln

Manager Macdonald and scorer Brown celebrate promotion.

The players acknowledge the crowd's cheers after the Lincoln game.

came back and scrambled an equaliser through Carr in the 72nd minute and then bombarded the Fulham goal for the remainder of the game. They came closest when O'Driscoll had to clear off the line but Fulham held on. With Burnley and Carlisle both winning their last games, Lincoln missed out on promotion, Fulham finished third and Burnley took the title. Despite missing out on top spot, ecstatic Fulham fans invaded the pitch and the players took a bow on the balcony of the Cottage. It was a memorable climax to a memorable season.

Reflections

It a relatively short space of time, Macdonald had effected a remarkable change in Fulham's fortunes. With one exception, all the players were already at the club when he took over the previous year but he was able to change the atmosphere at the Cottage. Gone was the tension so evident under his predecessor. Instead, under Macdonald and Harford, the players enjoyed a new freedom, a sense of fun and enjoyment, and they revelled in it. Not only was it good to watch but it was successful as well and the only surprise was that they left it to the very last minute to win the promotion the quality of their play deserved.

Early in the season, the manager had decided on his best team. It meant there was no room for the likes of Greenaway, Hatter, Mahoney, Beck, Banton, Goodlass and Clement. Fulham relied on the 11 players who played in at least 30 of the games with the only changes forced by injury or the occasional suspension. Of the 12 key players (the usual 11 plus Lock), five were home grown and Brown, at £100,000, was by far the most expensive. And, most encouragingly, there was a steady stream of youngsters in the reserves waiting for their chance.

Macdonald liked to say he was building a team that would not only win promotion but which could compete at a higher level. He was proved right. With the single addition of another free transfer (Ray Houghton from West Ham), the same Fulham squad came within a whisker of promotion to the top flight the following season, and were effectively cheated out of it by outrageous hooliganism at Derby on the final day of 1982-83, to which the authorities turned a blind eye.

But what should have been the dawn of a new era for Fulham quickly faded. Chairman Clay was more interested in acquiring the ground for his own financial gain than he was investing in the team. Manager Macdonald was undone by indiscretions in his private life and within 18 months this once-in-a-generation team started to break up. Fulham would sink to the very depths of the League over the next 15 years before they were to claim the prize that seemed within their grasp in 1982.

Summary Statistics

End	Played	Points	Position
September	7	13	5th
October	13	21	7th
November	17	26	8th
December	19	32	4th
January	22	41	1st
February	27	48	2nd
March	33	46	3rd
April	40	69	2nd
Final	**46**	**78**	**3rd**

	Home	Away	Total
P	23	23	**46**
W	12	9	**21**
D	9	6	**15**
L	2	8	**10**
F	44	33	**77**
A	22	29	**51**
Pts	45	33	**78**

0 points v	*1 point v*	*2 points v*	*3 points v*	*4 points v*	*6 points v*
Plymouth	Gillingham	Burnley	Brentford	Bristol C	Bristol R
	Huddersfield	Lincoln C	Chesterfield	Reading	Carlisle U
	Millwall	Portsmouth	Doncaster R	Southend U	Chester
	Oxford U	Walsall	Exeter C		Newport C
					Preston NE
					Swindon T
					Wimbledon
0 points	**4 points**	**8 points**	**12 points**	**12 points**	**42 points**

The Promotion Squad: 1981-82

Gerry Peyton: Irish international goalkeeper Peyton was signed from Burnley in 1976, missed only two games in the promotion season and made 395 first-class appearances for Fulham. He ranks 16th on the club's all-time appearances list. Consistent and brave, he had a long playing career that took in 10 clubs (many on loan) before turning to coaching, first with Fulham and then at Arsenal.

Jeff Hopkins: A product of Fulham's youth scheme, the promotion season was Hopkins' first in the League side. He later switched from right-back to centre-half and made 257 appearances for Fulham before a transfer to Crystal Palace in 1988. A winner of 16 Welsh caps, he also played for Plymouth, Bristol Rovers and Reading before finishing his career and settling in Australia.

Les Strong: Captain Strong was reaching the veteran stage, having made his debut in 1972. He was the only player to have played throughout the Campbell era and was made captain by Macdonald. Originally a right-winger, he switched to left-back and his 424 appearances for Fulham is the ninth highest total in the club's history. Hugely popular with supporters, Strong is still a matchday regular at the Cottage.

Sean O'Driscoll: Signed by Campbell from non-League Alvechurch in 1980, O'Driscoll blossomed into a classy and effective right sided midfield player under Macdonald. A quiet character, nicknamed 'Noisy' by skipper Strong, he won three Irish caps before moving to Bournemouth in 1984. He played over 500 games for the Cherries before he became manager in 2000. He has since managed Doncaster and is now at Nottingham Forest.

Roger Brown: An inspirational figure, Brown was signed from First Division Norwich in 1980 and was a pivotal member of the promotion side, up front with 12 goals, as well as at the back. A late entrant to the professional ranks (aged 25), he started with Bournemouth, and went back there after 161 games for Fulham. He had a brief foray in management with Colchester before working in the probation service. Brown was sadly a victim of cancer in 2011 before he was 60.

Tony Gale: Probably the outstanding product of Fulham's youth scheme over the last 40 years, Gale was in the League side in 1977 as a 17-year-old. He settled in the back four where he developed into a skilful and cultured defender, who lacked only real pace. He played 318 games for the Cottagers before moving to West Ham, where he made 268 appearances. He then teamed up with his old mentor Ray Harford at Blackburn where he won a Premiership medal. Gale now works as an analyst for Sky Television.

Gordon Davies: In two spells at the Cottage (either side of a couple of years at Chelsea and Manchester City), Davies scored a club record 178 goals in 450 outings. Another late entrant, the former schoolteacher signed for Fulham at the age of 22 in 1978, made his debut within a month and was a regular scorer thereafter. A Welsh international, he finished his League career at Wrexham, tried management in Norway but today runs his own business. He is also a match day regular at the Cottage today.

Robert Wilson: Fulham-born Wilson signed as a 16-year-old apprentice in 1977 and made his debut a few months after turning professional in 1979. A competitive midfield player who had the knack of making late runs into the penalty to score some useful goals, he had two spells at Fulham making 253 appearances in total. He also played for Millwall, Luton, Huddersfield and Rotherham and has settled in Yorkshire.

Dean Coney: A wonderfully talented striker much admired by Malcolm Macdonald, Coney came through the Fulham juniors and made his full debut in 1981. He developed an excellent partnership with Davies, and Coney scored 19 goals in his first full season. He went on to score 72 in 246 games for Fulham before his transfer to QPR in 1987. An England Under-21 player, he moved to Norwich in 1989 but was forced to leave League football through injury in 1991. He later featured in non-League football for Farnborough and Carshalton.

Peter O'Sullivan: Manager Macdonald's only signing, the experienced O'Sullivan, went to Fulham after 11 years and almost 500 games for Brighton. A Welsh international, he was a vital member of the Cottagers promotion side, although under-rated by the crowd. His work rate, control, distribution and tactical knowledge helped his younger colleagues and gave the team extra options down the left flank. It was his only season at the Cottage after which he played for Charlton, Reading and Aldershot before dropping into non-League football and working in financial services.

1981-82

League Division Three   Manager : Malcolm Macdonald

No		Date	V	Opponents	R	H-T	F-T	Scorers	Attend
1	A	29	H	Brentford	L	1-2	1-2	Davies	7,671
2	S	5	A	Lincoln C	D	0-0	1-1	Beck	3,034
3		12	H	Bristol C	W	0-1	2-1	Davies, Brown	4,169
4		19	A	Chesterfield	L	0-0	0-3		4,019
5		22	A	Wimbledon	W	1-0	3-1	Coney 2, Davies	5,554
6		26	H	Chester	W	2-0	2-0	O'Driscoll, Lewington	3,629
7		29	H	Southend U	W	0-1	2-1	Davies, Wilson	4,556
8	O	3	A	Oxford U	L	0-1	0-2		4,244
9		10	A	Huddersfield T	L	0-1	0-1		8,258
10		17	H	Newport C	W	1-1	3-1	Davies 2, Lewington	3,918
11		20	H	Exeter C	W	2-1	4-1	Davies 2, O'Driscoll, Brown	4,500
12		24	A	Burnley	D	0-2	2-2	Davies 2	4,224
13		31	H	Portsmouth	D	0-0	1-1	Wilson	7,542
14	N	3	A	Plymouth A	L	0-1	1-3	Davies	4,915
15		7	A	Carlisle U	W	2-0	2-1	Davies, Coney	4,385
16		14	H	Walsall	D	1-1	1-1	Brown	6,168
17		28	H	Millwall	D	0-0	0-0		8,343
18	D	5	A	Bristol R	W	1-0	2-1	Coney, Davies	4,489
19		30	A	Swindon T	W	2-0	4-1	Davies 2, Lock, O'Driscoll	5,641
20	J	20	A	Reading	W	2-0	3-0	Gale, Coney, Lewington	3,762
21		23	A	Brentford	W	0-0	1-0	O'Sullivan	10,830
22		30	H	Chesterfield	W	1-0	1-0	Davies	9,213
23	F	6	A	Bristol C	D	0-0	0-0		9,228
24		9	H	Wimbledon	W	1-0	4-1	Coney 2, Wilson, (Downes og)	7,802
25		19	A	Southend U	D	0-0	0-0		7,715
26		23	H	Oxford U	D	0-0	0-0		5,959
27		27	H	Huddersfield T	D	0-1	2-2	Coney, Lock	5,963
28	M	7	A	Newport C	W	0-0	3-1	Brown, Wilson, Coney	5,178
29		10	A	Exeter C	L	0-0	0-1		3,367
30		13	H	Burnley	D	1-1	1-1	Davies	7,124
31		16	H	Plymouth A	L	1-2	1-3	Tempest	5,105
32		20	A	Portsmouth	D	0-1	1-1	Lock	10,712
33		27	H	Carlisle U	W	3-0	4-1	Brown 2, Davies, O'Driscoll	7,477
34	A	3	A	Walsall	D	0-0	1-1	O'Driscoll	3,120
35		6	H	Doncaster R	W	1-1	3-1	Coney, Davies, Brown	5,081
36		10	A	Gillingham	L	0-1	0-2		9,985
37		13	H	Swindon T	W	2-0	2-0	Brown 2	6,655
38		17	H	Bristol R	W	2-0	4-2	Davies, Lock, Brown, O'Driscoll	6,849
39		20	A	Preston NE	W	1-1	3-1	Davies 2, Lock	6,009
40		25	A	Millwall	L	0-2	3-4	Brown, O'Driscoll, (Stevens og)	6,484
41	M	1	H	Reading	D	0-1	2-2	Wilson, Lewington	6,773
42		5	A	Chester	W	1-0	2-0	Coney, Tempest	1,174
43		8	A	Doncaster R	L	1-1	1-2	Coney	4,729
44		11	H	Gillingham	D	0-0	0-0		7,174
45		15	H	Preston NE	W	2-0	3-0	Davies 2, Coney	7,585
46		18	H	Lincoln C	D	0-0	1-1	Brown	20,398

Apps
Sub
Goals

				FA CUP					
1	N	21	A	Bristol R	W	0-0	2-1	Coney 2	6,497
2	J	2	A	Hereford U	L	0-1	0-1		4,619
				LEAGUE CUP					
1/1	S	1	A	Bournemouth	W	1-0	1-0	Davies	3,935
1/2		15	H	Bournemouth	W	0-0	2-0	Beck, Wilson	3,583
2/1	O	7	A	Newcastle U	W	0-0	2-1	Wilson, Coney	20,242
2/2		27	H	Newcastle U	W	1-0	2-0	Lewington, Coney	7,210
3	N	10	A	Oldham A	D	1-0	1-1	Wilson	6,619
R		17	H	Oldham A	W	2-0	3-0	Coney 2, Hopkins	6,985
4	D	2	A	Tottenham H	L	0-1	0-1		30,124

Peyton	Hopkins	Strong	Beck	Brown	Banton	Davies	Day	Coney	O'Sullivan	Lewington	Wilson	Gale	O'Driscoll	Scott	Tempest	Peters	Lock	Reeves	Parker	Stannard	#
1	2	3	4	5	6	7	8*	9	10	11	12										1
1	2	3	4	5		7	S	9	10	11	8	6									2
1	2	3	4	5		7		9	10	11	8	6						S			3
1	2	3	4	5		7	S	9	10	11	8	6									4
1	2	3		5		7	S	9	10	11	8	6	4								5
1	2	3		5		7	S	9	10	11	8	6	4								6
1	2	3		5		7	S	9	10	11	8	6	4								7
1	2	3		5		7	12	9	10	11	8	6	4*								8
1	2	3		5		7	12	9	10		8	6	4*	11							9
1	2	3		5		7	S	9	10	11	8	6	4								10
1	2	3		5		7	S	9	10	11	8	6	4								11
1	2	3		5		7	S		10	11	8	6	4		9						12
1	2	3		5		7	S	9	10	11	8	6	4								13
1	2	3		5		7		9	10	11	8	6	4*			12					14
1	2	3		5		7		9	10	11	8	6	4						S		15
1	2	3		5*		7	12	9	10	11	8	6	4								16
1	2	3		5		7		9	10	11	8	6	4				S				17
1	2	3		5		7		9	10	11	8	6	4				S				18
1	2	3		5		7		9*	10	11	8	6	4				12				19
1		3		5		7*		9	10	11			6	4			2	8	12		20
1		3		5				9	10	11			6	4		7	2	8	S		21
1		3		5		7*		9	10	11	8	6	4		12		2				22
1		3		5				9	10	11	8	6	4		7		2	S			23
1		3		5		7		9	10	11	8	6	4		S		2				24
1	12	3		5		7		9	10	11*	8	6	4				2				25
1		3		5		7		9	10		8	6	4*				2	11	12		26
1	S	3		5		7		9	10		8	6	4				2	11			27
1	S	3		5		7		9	10		8	6	4				2	11			28
1	S	3		5		7		9	10		8	6	4				2	11			29
1	12	3		5		7		9	10		8	6	4				2	11*			30
1	2	3	12	5		7				10	8		4*		9		6		11		31
1	2	3		5		7				10	8	6	4		9*		11		12		32
1	2	3		5		7				10	8	6	4		9		11		S		33
1	2	3		5		7		9			8	6	4		S		11		10		34
1	2	3		5		7		9	10		8	6	4		S		11				35
1	2	3		5		7		9	10		8	6	4		S		11				36
1	2	3		5		7		9	10		8	6	4		S		11				37
1	2	3		5		7		9	10		8	6	4		S		11				38
	2	3		5		7		9	10		8	6	4		S		11			1	39
	2	3		5*		7		9	10	8		6	4		12		11			1	40
1		2		5		7*		9	10	11	8	6	4		12		3				41
1	12	2		5				9	10	11	8	6*	4		7		3				42
1	S	2		5				9	10	11	8	6	4		7		3				43
1	12	2		5				9	10	11	8	6	4		7		3*				44
1	2	3*		5		7		9	10	11	8	6	4		12						45
1	2	3*		5		7		9	10	11	8	6	4		12						46

Peyton	Hopkins	Strong	Beck	Brown	Banton	Davies	Day	Coney	O'Sullivan	Lewington	Wilson	Gale	O'Driscoll	Scott	Tempest	Peters	Lock	Reeves	Parker	Stannard	
44	31	46	4	46	1	41	1	42	45	31	42	44	42	1	9	-	25	7	2	2	A
-	4	-	1	-	-	-	3	-	-	-	1	-	-	-	5	1	1	-	3	-	S
-	-	-	1	12	-	24	-	13	1	4	5	1	7	-	2	-	5	-	-	-	G

Peyton	Hopkins	Strong	Beck	Brown	Banton	Davies	Day	Coney	O'Sullivan	Lewington	Wilson	Gale	O'Driscoll	Scott	Tempest	Peters	Lock	Reeves	Parker	Stannard	
1	2	3*		5		7		9	10	11	8	6						12			1
1	2	3		5		7		9	10	11	8	6						S			2

Peyton	Hopkins	Strong	Beck	Brown	Banton	Davies	Day	Coney	O'Sullivan	Lewington	Wilson	Gale	O'Driscoll	Scott	Tempest	Peters	Lock	Reeves	Parker	Stannard	
1	2	3	4	5		7	S	9	10	11	8	6									1/1
1	2	3	4	5		7	S	9	10	11	8	6									1/2
1	2	3		5		7		9	10	11*	8	6	4					12			2/1
1	2	3		5		7	S	9	10	11	8	6	4								2/2
1	2	3		5		7		9	10	11	8	6	4					S			3
1	2	3				7	S	9	10	11	8	6	4					5			R
1	2	3		5		7		9	10	11	8	6	4					S			4

Ray Lewington: Another 1980 signing by Campbell, Lewington arrived at Fulham from Wimbledon but had made his name earlier at Chelsea. Few people have contributed as much in so many roles at the Cottage, as player, manager, coach, development manager, etc. right up to 2012. He also played for Sheffield United and coached or managed Palace, Brentford and Watford. Lewington is today assistant to Roy Hodgson in the England management hierarchy.

Kevin Lock: Used as cover for virtually all defensive positions and in midfield, Lock was stylish and dependable, the possessor of an accurate left foot, and perhaps the club's best-ever penalty taker. He was the outstanding player on the pitch in the 1975 Cup Final – but for West Ham. Lock joined Fulham three years later and made 222 appearances, a total which would have been higher but for injuries. He moved on to Southend in 1985, where he was also involved in the coaching. He also coached at Chelsea and Millwall and was assistant manager at Brentford but left football in the 1990s.

6.

The Adams Family: 1996-97

Fulham's long slide to near-oblivion began in the mid-1980s. The cash-strapped chairman Ernie Clay sold off the best players and concentrated his energies on buying the ground with a view to building on it. Following relegation in 1986 to the (old) Third Division, Clay sold out to a property company who proposed merging the Cottagers with one of their other 'assets', QPR, with the new club playing at Loftus Road. Jimmy Hill, a former Fulham player, led a public outcry and ended up fronting a small group which bought the club but not the ground in 1987. There were many twists and turns behind the scenes over the next few years but on the pitch, the club sank like a stone. After several near misses, they dropped into the League basement for the first time in 1994.

It got worse before it got better. In February 1996, Fulham were next to bottom of what was now the Third Division, in reality the Fourth. They were 91st out of 92 clubs in the League and staring the Vauxhall Conference in the face. Between 1987 and 1996 managers came and went. The unlucky Lewington made way for the incompetent Alan Dicks who then was succeeded by the equally clueless Don Mackay. By the time they reach the lowest division, Ian Branfoot, once of Reading and South-ampton, was in charge. A disciplinarian who did little to make himself popular with the supporters, Branfoot brought some order and structure to the playing side, but with no discernible improvements in results. With his team languishing one place off the bottom of the entire League, he stepped aside, took on the General Manager's role and handed over team responsibilities to a young protégée.

Among the players Branfoot had signed for Fulham was one of football's nomadic journeymen, full-back Micky Adams. In a career that stretched back to 1978, he had played for Gillingham, Coventry, Leeds, Southampton and Stoke and in 1994, by then in his early thirties, Adams was looking to get involved in coaching. He had played for Branfoot at the Dell and he was brought to Fulham with the title of 'player-coach'. In his first season, however, he still made a big contribution on the playing side, with 11 goals. He was second highest scorer behind Simon Morgan, although most of Adams' goals were from free-kicks or penalties. But injuries were limiting his appearances and when it was clear a change was needed at the top, Adams was on the spot to take over from Branfoot in February 1996.

Without doubt it was a gamble for a club in such a precarious position. The new man had no previous managerial experience, was one of the youngest managers in the League and was being asked to manage players who were essentially teammates. But, having said all that, he succeeded, not only in keeping Fulham in the League in 1995-96 but also in steering them to the club's first promotion for 15 years in his first full season in charge. He did it with a group of players comprising veterans, free transfers and promising youngsters. He had very little to work with but made the

The promotion team group. Back row, left to right: Angus, Blake, Walton, Cullip, Lange, Stewart, Mison. Middle row: Chris Smith (physio), Freeman, Thomas, McAree, Barkus, Honor, Hamill, Watson, Hamsher, Herrera, Scott, John Marshall (youth team coach). Front row: Grover, Cockerill, Cusack, Len Walker (assistant manager), Micky Adams (player-manager), Alan Cork (reserve team coach), Morgan, Conroy, Brooker.

most of it. There was a collective spirit at the club for the first time in years, created by Adams and his assistant Alan Cork. Neither was at the forefront of tactical thinking, there was no money to spend and the backstage manoeuvrings were coming to a climax and were a big distraction.

Yet Adams, for all his lack of experience, coped admirably and set Fulham on the road that led to the Premiership within four years. For reasons he understood and accepted, his part in Fulham's rise ended with promotion from the League's lowest tier. In many ways, it was the most difficult of the three promotions Fulham were to achieve in the next three years and without it, it is doubtful whether the Fayed Revolution would even have got off the ground. Adams skill was old-fashioned management, the ability to weld together players with disparate skills from a wide variety of backgrounds and to get more out of them than most others would have done. If the whole was greater than the sum of the parts, it was because of Adams ability to create a family unit that held together over a long 46-match season.

Having steered the Cottagers clear of the dreaded drop zone in his first months in the job, Adams spent the summer of 1996 restructuring his squad. He knew it was not good enough but he had very little cash at his disposal. He needed to perform a financial balancing act. So, seven players went out (Gary Brazil, Duncan Jupp, Lee Harrison, Danny Bolt, Danny Bower, Carl Williams and Kevin Moore) and seven came in, the most significant of whom were Darren Freeman and Paul Watson (both from Gillingham), Danny Cullip (previously with Oxford), goalkeeper Mark Walton (rescued from non-League football), and the veteran Glenn Cockerill, freed by

Orient but an old playing colleague of Adams at Southampton. Simon Morgan continued to captain the side but Nick Cusack was switched successfully to sweeper. The other survivors from the previous season included Mark Blake, Terry Angus, Robbie Herrera, Micky Conroy and Rob Scott.

Compared to previous and future promotion winning sides, it was a bit of a hotch potch squad, a make-do-and-mend team which perhaps surprised itself as much as it did the supporters. But, unknown to most people, it got off to a cracking start with a pre-season

Manager Adams in his first full season in charge.

Morgan scores number three against Colchester in September.

The winning goal at Exeter was a header by Freeman, his first for the club.

tour of the Republic of Ireland, a trip to Cornwall and rousing talks from a positive and confidant Adams. By the time of the first game in August, spirits among the players was high and a self-belief established that had been missing previously. This was reflected in the brightest start to a League campaign the club had made for over a decade.

In Front From the Start

A real test awaited Fulham on the opening day, a visit from Hereford, a side which had made the Play-offs the previous May. There was no Cockerill, Angus or Freeman but there were debuts for Walton, Watson and Cullip and rare outings for Mison and McAree. The crowd of 5,277 was the division's largest that day and they had to wait 55 minutes for what proved to be the winning goal. A Watson corner was flicked on by Cusack at the near post for Conroy to stab in. It was the first strike in what was to be a purple patch for Conroy whose tally for the season was the highest by a Fulham player for 13 years. There were other chances, but the one goal was enough for the points.

Next up were two away games, at Hartlepool and midweek at Rochdale and Fulham were as lucky to win the second of these games as they were unlucky to lose the first. In the north east, 37-year-old Cockerill played his first game, the oldest player ever to make his Fulham debut. The hosts went in front on 58 minutes, a shot by former Fulham player Cooper taking a deflection. Although Scott equalised 11 minutes later following a Watson corner, Hartlepool scored a breakaway goal through Davies eight minutes from time. This after a Blake header was cleared off the line, Morgan hit the post and Freeman had a goal disallowed. At Spotland, Cusack was on the mark following a long throw by Scott and although Rochdale piled on the pressure, Conroy increased the Cottagers lead on 68 minutes with a diving header. Rochdale did deservedly pull one back with 10 minutes to go, but it was not enough.

It was too early to take the League table seriously after three games but it is interesting to note that the three sides that won promotion in May all featured in the top five, Wigan, Carlisle and Fulham. And one of those teams, Carlisle, were the next visitors to the Cottage. It took Conroy only eight minutes to make it three goals in four games, a header across the goal at the Putney End. Although there were chances at both ends in the remaining 82 minutes, there were no more goals. By winning the next three games, at home to Colchester (3-1), away at Exeter (1-0) and at Swansea (2-1), the Cottagers made it six wins in seven games, and five on the trot. Conroy got half of the six-goal haul, skipper Morgan two and there was a first goal from Freeman, the winner at Exeter. His long hair and mazy runs were already making the eccentric Freeman a crowd favourite.

Fulham were worthy winners in all three matches and coming back from behind at Swansea showed the character that was in the team. For the first time in more than a decade, Fulham topped a League table but they were brought down to earth with a bump by Mansfield, a side that had yet to win a game and which had not scored for 395 minutes. The Stags had a 2-0 lead before Morgan found the net in the last minute. A re-shuffle because of an injury to Cockerill was some excuse but Adams thought the team should have done better. It was a chastening experience, although they bounced back the next week with a very professional win at Darlington. Another Gillingham old boy, Richard Carpenter was signed in midweek and scored the second in a 2-0 win, a fierce drive in the last minute. He was also involved in the first goal when he was fouled in the 33rd minute and Watson scored with an exquisite curling free-kick. But there was more bad news when Torquay won in midweek at the Cottage, a match Fulham totally dominated but could not finish off. Although Scott scored in the first half, two Nelson goals late in the game meant two successive home defeats for Adams' team.

Autumn Sunshine

Still second after 10 games, Fulham nevertheless could not afford too many slips against teams like Mansfield and Torquay, and between the start of October and the end of the year, there was only one, again at home, to mid-table Lincoln. Managed by former Fulham player John Beck, the Imps were a big, physical side that played direct football. The Cottagers were undone after just five minutes and although Carpenter equalised on the half hour, the visitors took the points with a typical headed goal 10 minutes from time.

This defeat came early in November after a run five wins and a draw in October and then four wins and four draws in the last eight games of 1996. For the whole of the last three months of the year, Fulham topped the table.

There were some very impressive performances in this sequence. The 1-0 win at Northampton was better than it sounded, Conroy was again on the mark, and the home game against Doncaster, on the 100th anniversary of the first match at the Cottage, which contained spectacular second half goals by Scott and Carpenter after the almost obligatory header from Conroy. When Cambridge visited SW6 days later, they were second in the table on a six-match winning run. They were blitzed by three goals in the opening half, two from Conroy and a Blake penalty. There was another 3-0 win a few days later, at Hull, which meant six away victories on the trot. Freeman, Watson and Conroy were on the scoresheet, although it might have been different if Hull had made the most of their early possession. A point from a trip to Brighton was, in the manager's view, a point won not two dropped and he was positively purring following the 2-1 midweek win over Scunthorpe. After the visitors had taken an early lead, Morgan and Cusack both hit a post before Conroy equalised after 25 minutes with a curling shot. The winner did not come until the 68th minute, Freeman curling the ball inside the post from an acute angle. Adams thought this was as well as his team had played all season, a very good all-round performance.

There were three wins in the four games immediately after the Lincoln defeat which kept the Cottagers in pole position. Like Cambridge, Cardiff had won their previous six matches before meeting Fulham at Ninian Park, and, as against the 'U's', Fulham were more than equal to the task. Adams described the 2-1 win as 'thoroughly professional', which understated the extent of his team's dominance. It took less than a minute to get ahead, Conroy (inevitably) diving to head in Scott's cross. The second came on 34 minutes when Scott dispossessed old Fulham favourite Eckhardt and was bundled over as he raced for goal. Blake scored from the spot. Although the Bluebirds got a late consolation through White, the result was never in doubt.

Before Fulham entertained Barnet in a midweek match, they were dumped out of the FA Cup 5-0 at Plymouth. It was a real thrashing by one of the previous season's promoted sides, an ominous sign for the next season perhaps, but at the time nobody really minded the early Cup exit. And the performance against Barnet showed that in the League, it was business as usual. A goal in either half, by Conroy and Morgan, took care of the North London side, managed that night by Alan Mullery.

Few people could have anticipated the significance of top-of-the-table Fulham's visit to third-placed Wigan the following Saturday. In near arctic conditions on a snow-bound pitch and without the injured Conroy, Fulham were given a helping hand when the Latics' striker Jones was sent off for butting Angus after 38 minutes (the second time he had been red carded against the Cottagers). But the 10 men pushed forward and took a 58th minute lead through a certain Roberto Martinez. Only when Paul Brooker came on as a substitute for Cockerill did Fulham threaten and he was instrumental in setting up Scott's late equaliser. Had Fulham managed to take all three points against a depleted Wigan, they rather than the Latics would have been champions in May. Fulham returned to winning ways on the last day of November with a 2-0 win at home to Brighton, both goals coming in the second half, from Conroy (a header from another Watson cross) and a Blake penalty, awarded for a foul on Conroy. It might, however, have been very different if Tony Lange had not saved Maskell's 26th minute penalty following a Cockerill foul.

Winter Draws On

Although the Cottagers kept their unbeaten run going until the end of the year, they dropped points in December, drawing matches they might have been expected to win. As a result, the eight point lead at the top they held after the Brighton victory had narrowed to one point at the turn of the year. There were only 1,762 people on a wintry night at Chester to see Fulham set a new club record of 10 unbeaten away games on the trot. It was a game that came to life only in the last half hour. The match was played in a swirling wind and then driving rain, which added to the late drama. Chester's Priest got sent off just after the hour for two yellow cards and then, four minutes later, Morgan followed, with a straight red. Rather than the free-kick Fulham were expecting, the referee awarded a penalty to Chester, which Peter Reid's brother, Shaun, converted. Even if the penalty award was right, the red card was clearly wrong for it was Carpenter not Morgan who committed the offence (and served the subsequent suspension). The visitors rescued a point when Freeman came on as a substitute for Herrera and he scored with a header from a Watson corner. The linesman adjudged the ball had crossed the line before a defender cleared.

Against Orient at home, Fulham faced 47-year-old Peter Shilton in his 999th League game. The holder of a record number of England caps showed that goal-keepers can have a longer shelf life than other players and he denied Conroy on a least six occasions with top-class saves. It took a spectacular effort from Watson standing at the edge of the box to beat him. The Cottagers went 1-0 up in the 65th and then Orient had McGleish sent off and the three points looked safe. But in injury time, the Fulham defence failed to clear a free-kick and Warren headed an equaliser. Carelessness had cost Adams team two valuable points. Another two were wasted in the next home game, on Boxing Day against Exeter. Despite dominating the game (13 corners and 17 shots on goal), Fulham had to settle for another 1-1 draw, and to make matters worse, Angus scored both goals. He put Exeter in front with an unfortunate deflection after 26 minutes and then equalised a quarter of an hour later with a header from Watson's cross.

Either side of the Exeter game were two victories, a competent midweek win at Scarborough and a season's best score of 6-0 at home to Darlington. Watson was involved in both goals at Scarborough, Conroy heading in a cross from the right on the quarter of an hour mark and then Morgan, two minutes before half-time, completing the scoring when the defence failed to clear another cross from the full-back. Herrera was injured for this game, and Adams picked himself for his first start in 15 months. He subbed himself early in the second half. The most remarkable feature of the Darlington win (apart from seeing Paul Parker in a Fulham shirt for the first time in a decade – he had been signed on a short-term contract) was that the six goals came from six different scorers. Even without Cusack and Blake, Fulham overwhelmed a Quakers side that had come to the Cottage to attack, but got found out.

Rather than signal a return to the form of the autumn, the thrashing of Darlington marked a peak before a dip in performances and results that led to four defeats in the next five games, the club's worst run of the season. Fulham surrendered top spot in the table by the beginning of February and although they had a three-point margin over Carlisle, the Cumbrian side had two games in hand. The slide in January meant the chasing pack had closed the gap.

There was an amusing sideshow to the defeat at Colchester which followed days after the win over Darlington. Fulham supporters leaving the Cottage by coach for the Tuesday evening game had a new driver, who was aware that the match was against a team beginning with the letter 'C' to the east of London. His passengers were not best pleased to be taken to Cambridge rather than Colchester, arriving too later to get to Layer Road once he realised the mistake. Those supporters probably got off lightly. On a bone-hard pitch, the Cottagers lost their first away game since August after a lethargic first half display and a controversial decision in the second. The home side took a 42nd minute lead, which was equalised by Morgan just after the hour following one of Scott's long throws. An off-the-ball challenge on Scott led to Colchester's Greene seeing red and against 10 men, Fulham were well on top. When the home goalkeeper handled outside the box, he was shown only a yellow rather than a red card and shortly afterwards Adam's men conceded the winning goal when Fry was allowed to run unchallenged before shooting past Lange.

An away defeat at Torquay 12 months earlier had marked the lowest point in Fulham's history and sparked the changes that led to Adams' promotion. Yet again, Plainmoor proved to be a bogey ground, despite a promising start. Scott had given Fulham a 38th minute lead with a far post header but then, two minutes before half-time, Herrera dislocated a shoulder. With Angus switching to left-back and Cullip coming on in the middle of defence, the balance of the side was upset, and Torquay took full advantage. In nine second half minutes, Fulham conceded an equaliser, a contentious penalty and a third, decisive goal, two headers and a spot kick, to record successive away defeats for the first time.

The players picked themselves up after this defeat and gave superb performance at Scunthorpe. Cusack put the Cottagers ahead after only four minutes, which was followed by a sublime Conroy volley (32 minutes) and a Blake penalty (40) after a foul on Freeman. Scott rounded off an exhilarating display in the 82nd minute with a clever hook shot just a couple of minutes after Scunthorpe had a got a consolation goal. But any hopes this win marked the turning of the corner were dashed the following Friday, when Cardiff visited the Cottage for a match that was shown live on Sky. It was a meeting between the division's highest scorers and a Cardiff team that had gone 365 minutes of away football without scoring.

Fulham blew the chance to showcase their talents. They started without regular wing backs Watson (suspended) and Herrera (injured) and had Adams and Parker deputising. It was the last Fulham appearance for both players. It was a thoroughly inept team performance. Cardiff led 1-0 at the interval when Fowler lobbed Lange after half an hour. Within 10 minutes of the re-start, it was 3-0, two goals resulting from White taking advantage of sloppy defending. Although former Fulham man Eckhardt thoughtfully reduced the arrears with an own-goal, White restored the Bluebirds three-goal advantage five minutes from time.

It really looked as though the wheels were coming off the promotion push when a week later Fulham went down 2-0 at Sincil Bank. Mid-table Lincoln had won at the Cottage in the autumn and completed the double with a 2-0 win at the start of February. It was also Lincoln manager John Beck's fourth win in five meetings with his old club. Adams had signed two loan players to strengthen his squad, Charlie Hartfield from Sheffield United and Matt Lawrence from Wycombe, and both started against the Imps but the slump continued. Ainsworth gave the home side the lead on 22 minutes and Fulham old boy Phil Stant sealed the outcome in the 79th minute, lobbing the advancing Walton.

Light at the End of the Tunnel

Taking just three points from a possible 15 was hardly promotion form and Fulham had to reverse the decline very quickly. Adams talked a good game but it was a bit of luck on a cold Tuesday evening in front of fewer than 5,000 at the Cottage that prove to be a turning point. Had Fulham lost this game, there would have been just two points between them and that evening's visitors, fourth-placed Swansea. And, when the Swans went a goal up in the 53rd minute, many thought that was on the cards. The goal came against the run of play. A Watson corner was charged down and Fulham got hit on the break, Coates finishing off the move. But it was no surprise when the Cottagers got back on terms 10 minutes later when Freeman netted from close range. It was not until four minutes from time that they got the vital goal. Goalkeeper Freestone parried Conroy's lob in the air and substitute Brooker followed up to volley in a match-winning and season-saving goal. An ecstatic Adams was full of praise for his team afterwards, highlighting their patience, resilience and work rate.

Wigan was another potential six-pointer days later but ended as a two-pointer, with the honours shared. The score at the Cottage was the same as at Springfield Park in November, 1-1, and there was nothing between the teams in the two games between them or over the 46-match season. With Martinez again running the midfield, Lowe put the Latics ahead in the 52nd minutes, but a hotly disputed penalty awarded when Conroy went over, gave Blake the chance to equalise from the spot, which he accepted.

There were now nine points between top-of-the-table Fulham and Swansea in fourth place, and the Swans had played a game more. With Carlisle and Wigan in second and third spot, the final lap of the season looked like becoming a battle for the title, with the three leaders seeming comfortable for promotion. March ended with a full-blooded London derby at Barnet. Fulham came back from behind twice to earn a point but the two dropped cost them top spot. After Conroy had equalised Hodges opener in the 29th minute, the Cottagers' talisman was stretchered off with an ankle injury. On the hour, the Bees went ahead through a penalty awarded for reasons only referee Rennie understood. Wilson scored. Substitute Scott levelled after 68 minutes, touching in Freeman's cross, but Fulham still felt they were worth three points on the day.

McAree's vital winning goal at Carlisle which virtually clinched promotion.

Into The Home Straight

And so the Cottagers went into the final two months of the season in good spirits, well entrenched in the promotion places with just 12 games to go. March was a good month. Of the six League games, four were won and two drawn and the end of it, Fulham were nine points clear of fourth place, with a game in hand. They needed just seven points from their last six games to be mathematically certain of going up. With a game in hand on leaders Wigan, and just one point behind, they knew the divisional Championship was within their grasp. More and more it was looking as though the match away at Carlisle at the beginning of April would be the big one.

But each game before that mattered and the draw at home to Chester was a disappointment. The visitors were chasing a Play-off place, but the game was a tepid affair. A rare error by Morgan gave Chester the lead after half an hour although the skipper redeemed himself with the equaliser just before the hour mark. Without Conroy, however, they lacked punch up front. He was still absent for the visit of Scarborough a week later but this time others stepped up to the scoring plate. Fulham had loan signing Christer Warren from Southampton making his debut but it was another Southampton old boy, Cockerill, who opened the scoring after just two minutes with his only goal for the club. He was on hand for Scott's pull back from the right. Within four minutes it was 2-0, thanks to a typically individual Freeman effort. Freeman was the man-of-the-match. He was brought down for the penalty which Blake converted on 66 minutes and he provided the cross for Warren's debut goal 10 minutes later.

A Sunday journey to Brisbane Road was next, the day after Carlisle lost and Wigan only drew. With yet another Blake penalty (Freeman again fouled) and a Carpenter close range effort, both late in the game, Fulham equalled the club record of 10 away wins in a season as well as closing the gap on leaders Carlisle. Conroy returned for the visit of Hartlepool, but only as a substitute. But it was Freeman, enjoying his best form of the season, who scored the only goal. He got on the end of a Lawrence cross and placed a firm header past O'Connor on the half hour for the only goal of a rather dull match. The dismissal of 'Pool's Beech after 58 minutes was the only real excitement of the second half. Against bottom-of-the-table Hereford, the Cottagers maintained their record of never having won at Edgar Street. There were some near misses, all at the Hereford end, but a goalless draw was all they could manage. It was the same at home against Rochdale a week later. A typical Conroy goal after 12 minutes, a near post header from a Warren cross, marked the striker's return to full

The second of Morgan's two goals against Hull.

Celebrating Fulham's first promotion for 15 years.

fitness but that was as good as it got for Fulham. A well-organised Rochdale side grabbed an equaliser before half-time through Gouck's long-range effort and much of the rest of the game was played out in midfield.

Perhaps the following week's visit to Carlisle was on the players' minds. Fulham were third, one point and one place behind Carlisle and on the same number of games (40). This could be a clincher for either team. Adams' team travelled north without Blake, Carpenter and Freeman and Irishman Rod McAree was given a rare outing in a three-man midfield. In what felt like a Cup tie atmosphere, Fulham trailed at half-time to a Delap header but the Cottagers took control of the second half. McAree crossed to the far post in the 51st minute for Cullip to head back across goal where Conroy was waiting to poach another goal. Just two minutes later, Warren knocked the ball into the path of McAree on the edge of the box and he ensured himself a place in Fulham folklore with a half-volley that flew into the corner of the net. Carlisle, who made a habit of scoring late in games, piled on the pressure but the Fulham defence coped comfortably. At the final whistle, supporters and players knew this was a famous win that all but guaranteed promotion.

Statistically, the guarantee came three days later at Field Mill in front of fewer than 5,000 people. Mansfield were not going to lie down and gift Fulham the three points. Both sides pushed for a winner but had to be happy with a goalless draw and at the final whistle, hundreds of jubilant supports ran on to the pitch. The players acknowledged their cheers from the Mansfield directors' box and then went on to party long into the night. Some had not shaken off the effects by the time they lined up against Northampton at the Cottage the next Saturday – and it showed. The division's biggest crowd of the season, 11,479, was in celebratory mood as Fulham pursued the divisional title. But the Cobblers were party poopers. After missing two acceptable chances, they scored after just seven minutes, White taking the ball half the length of the pitch before beating Walton. Adams substituted Angus and Lawrence within the first 20 minutes and was so annoyed at the first-half display, he sent the players back out on to the pitch after just five minutes of the interval. If they were embarrassed, it did little to improve their performance and the manager had no complaints about the 1-0 scoreline afterwards. He was angry enough to have them back in for training the next day, Sunday.

It must have done some good. Fulham did not concede a goal in the last three games, drawing in midweek at Doncaster, beating Hull at home thanks to two Morgan goals and then rounding off the season with a 1-0 win at Cambridge, a match settled by Freeman's 14th minute goal. He collected Conroy's pass and rounded 'keeper Barrett before slotting the ball home. Unfortunately, it was not enough. With two games to go, both Fulham and Wigan had 81 points, with Carlisle in third place on 78. The day Fulham beat Hull, the Latics defeated Torquay 3-0. So, on the final day, Fulham needed to do better than Wigan to finish in top spot. Beating Cambridge was a help but with Wigan beating Mansfield, the Cottagers had to settle for runners-up spot. Both clubs had 87 points, but the Latics had scored 84 goals to Fulham's 72.

That hangover against Northampton was an expensive one. Despite club records of 87 points and 12 away wins, the Cottagers missed out on their first silverware for nearly half a century by the narrowest of margins. Although there were a number of games in which points were squandered, the home defeat at the hands of Northampton, coming hard on the heels of the memorable victory at Carlisle and promotion-clinching draw at Mansfield, stands out. It was, nevertheless, a triumphant season achieved by an unlikely team. For Adams, in his first full season as a manger, it was a major personal success, all the more enjoyable because the initial expectations were so low. It was a success he was to repeat several times with other clubs at this level of the League. Fulham's fortunes were on an upward trajectory, but few people could have anticipated the speed of the future ascent.

Reflections

Although disappointed at not winning the divisional title, there was relief and joy at the Cottage that Fulham were no longer in the League basement. Against the odds, and in a relatively short space of time, manager Adams had turned a club fearful of dropping into non-League football into promotion winners, denied silverware only on goals scored (had it been goal difference or goal average the title would have gone to Fulham). He was justifiably selected as the Nationwide Division Three Manager of the Year.

This was, however, no ordinary year. Not only were there exciting developments on the field but there were major developments behind the scenes as well. The long-running saga over the ground was building to a climax. Following the takeover of one property company (Marler Estates) and the failure of another in the recession (Cabra Estates), Craven Cottage was owned by the Royal Bank of Scotland. Director Tom Wilson negotiated a purchase price and vice-chairman Bill Muddyman stretched his credit to pay for it. For the first time, Fulham owned their historic home, and in the season in which they won promotion, which was a problem as well as an opportunity.

Much of the ground was in poor condition and needed substantial sums spent on it. The team, good enough for promotion from Division Three, would probably struggle at a higher level and needed substantial sums spent on it. But the resources had been drained by the purchase of the ground and a White Knight was needed. Enter Mohamed Al Fayed, who subsequently proved to a fairy godfather rather than a mere white knight. But for Adams and his players, their prospects were transformed.

By Christmas 1997, seven months after promotion, Fulham had a new owner, a new board of directors, a new manager and a totally different playing squad. Adams reward for promotion, in effect, was the sack. Had he not been successful, Fayed may not have wanted to buy the club and Adams may have kept his job. But the new owner's revolutionised everything about Fulham, and unquestionably for the better, and so the supporters owe a great deal to Adams and his team who made Fulham a much more attractive purchase. Later, Adams was gracious enough to admit that he probably was not a big enough name for the new chairman and he would have found it difficult to persuade players from the Premiership to drop down a couple of divisions to play for Fulham, something which Kevin Keegan managed to do. But his contribution should not be under-estimated. Never was there more truth in the old saying, 'mighty oaks from little acorns'.

Summary Statistics

End	Played	Points	Position
September	9	21	1st
October	16	37	1st
November	21	47	1st
December	25	55	1st
January	30	59	1st
February	34	64	2nd
March	40	76	3rd
April	45	84	2nd
Final	**46**	**87**	**2nd**

	H	A	Total
P	23	23	**46**
W	13	12	**25**
D	5	7	**12**
L	5	4	**9**
F	41	31	**72**
A	20	18	**38**
Pts	44	43	**87**

0 points v	1 point v	2 points v	3 points v	4 points v	6 points v
Lincoln C	Mansfield T	Chester C	Cardiff C	Barnet	Cambridge U
Torquay U		Wigan A	Colchester U	Brighton & HA	Carlisle U
			Hartlepool U	Doncaster R	Darlington
			North'pton T	Exeter C	Hull C
				Hereford U	Scarborough
				Leyton O	Scunthorpe U
				Rochdale	Swansea C
0 points	**1 point**	**4 points**	**12 points**	**28 points**	**42 points**

The Promotion Squad: 1996-97

Mark Walton: Rescued from non-League football with Fakenham Town in 1996, Walton won the battle for the goalkeeper's jersey with Tony Lange. He had been with six other League clubs before Fulham and he fitted in well at the Cottage. The promotion campaign was his one full season at the club and like many of his team-mates moved on once Adams left. He later played for Brighton and Cardiff.

Paul Watson: Another of Adams close season signings, Fulham paid Gillingham a nominal fee for Watson, he missed only two games in the promotion run. A natural left footer, he played part of the season on the right and impressed with his surges down the flank, crosses and dead-ball kicking. Adams signed him twice more, for Brentford in December 1997 and Brighton in 1999.

Robbie Herrera: An attacking full-back, Herrera had played in the top flight for QPR before joining Fulham in 1994. He was one of the few survivors of the squad that had been relegated. He made 173 appearances for Fulham and when injury cost him his place the following season, Herrera returned to Torquay, his home-town club in 1998.

Danny Cullip: Freed by Oxford, the shaven-headed Cullip was a pacey, hard tackling central-defender who went straight into the first team at the age of 19. He played in 29 of the 46 League games in the promotion season but the arrival of Keegan spelt the end of his Fulham career. Adams signed him for Brentford in 1998 and again for

Brighton in 1999 once he had recovered from a broken leg. He helped the Seagulls to two promotions.

Nick Cusack: A much travelled player who had been with non-League, League and Scottish clubs, Cusack was 29 when he joined Fulham in 1995, initially as a striker. But Adams successfully converted him to sweeper, where his intelligent reading of the game compensated for a lack of pace. He followed Adams to Swansea in 1997 and was briefly manager in 2002. A graduate, he is now a full-time official of the PFA.

Mark Blake: Central-defender Blake was an early signing by manager Branfoot in 1994 and was Fulham's Player of the Year in his first season. A reliable and consistent central-defender who had also played for Southampton and Shrewsbury, he was the nominated penalty taker. Blake played a leading role in the promotion success, which he combined with studying for a Business Studies degree. After 161 appearances for the Cottagers, he left in 1998 to try his luck in France but returned to play in non-League football in Hampshire.

Terry Angus: A free transfer signing from Northampton in 1993, central-defender Angus endeared himself to the crowd with his wholehearted commitment and obvious enthusiasm for playing. A late entrant into professional football (he was 24 when he joined Northampton), he was released straight after the promotion season having played 137 times for Fulham. He went into non-League football, first with Slough and then Nuneaton Borough.

Micky Conroy: Fulham paid what for them was the not inconsiderable sum of £75,000 for Conroy in 1995. A proven scorer at Reading, Burnley and Preston, the 30-year-old Glaswegian disappointed in his first season at the Cottage but struck gold in his second. With 21 League goals, 16 before Christmas, he was the spearhead of the attack, and was lethal with his head and both feet. He did not survive the Keegan cull the following year and went back north to Blackpool and in 1999, emigrated to Australia.

Simon Morgan: The captain and inspiration, Morgan signed for Fulham in 1990 and made 408 appearances before teaming up with Adams again at Brighton in 2001. Primarily a central-defender, he played in most positions and three divisions of the League in 11 years at Fulham, and also contributed some useful goals, eight in the promotion season and 53 in his Fulham career. Morgan currently works as Head of Community development for the Premier League.

Rob Scott: Surrey-born Scott signed for Fulham from Sheffield United the month before Adams took over in 1996 for a very modest fee. A right sided midfield player or striker, he scored nine valuable goals in the promotion season, including several very spectacular strikes. He also possessed a very long throw. He fell out of favour when Adams left and moved to Rotherham in 1998.

Glenn Cockerill: Another free transfer, Cockerill was an old teammate of Adams from Southampton. At 37 he became the oldest player ever to make his Fulham debut but his experience made an important contribution in midfield. Cockerill had started with Lincoln and played against Fulham in the 1982 promotion decider. He then went to Sheffield United, had eight years at the Dell and 18 months at Orient before joining Fulham. He followed Adams to Brentford, where he was assistant manager, and was later assistant manager at Palace.

Darren Freeman: Signed for next-to-nothing from Gillingham in the 1996 close season, Freeman's exciting and unpredictable runs down the left flank unsettled defences and made him a crowd favourite. With more luck with injuries and better finishing, he could have been a top class player. Given a free by Fulham in 1998, he was in Brentford's promotion side under Adams the next season and again with Adams at Brighton in 2001.

Richard Carpenter: The third of the Gillingham trio signed by Adams, Carpenter did not arrive until the season was a month old. A strong runner with a powerful shot and accurate cross, he was a key player in midfield in the promotion run. Injuries held him back the following season and in 1998 he moved to Cardiff before linking up with Adams again in 2000, where he was involved in two more promotions.

			League Division Three			Manager : Micky Adams		

No		Date	V	Opponents	R	H-T	F-T	Scorers	Attend
1	A	17	H	Hereford U	W	0-0	1-0	Conroy	5,277
2		24	A	Hartlepool U	L	0-0	1-2	Scott	2,457
3		27	A	Rochdale	W	1-0	2-1	Cusack, Conroy	1,689
4		31	H	Carlisle U	W	1-0	1-0	Conroy	5,860
5	S	7	H	Colchester U	W	0-2	3-1	Conroy 2, Morgan	5,189
6		10	A	Exeter C	W	1-0	1-0	Freeman	2,388
7		14	A	Swansea C	W	0-1	2-1	Conroy, Morgan	3,791
8		21	H	Mansfield T	L	0-1	1-2	Morgan	5,740
9		28	A	Darlington	W	1-0	2-0	Watson, Carpenter	3,269
10	O	1	H	Torquay U	L	1-0	1-2	Scott	4,459
11		5	A	Northampton T	W	0-0	1-0	Conroy	6,171
12		12	H	Doncaster R	W	0-0	3-1	Conroy, Scott, Carpenter	5,516
13		15	H	Cambridge U	W	3-0	3-0	Conroy 2, Blake	5,791
14		19	A	Hull C	W	1-0	3-0	Freeman, Watson, Conroy	3,986
15		26	A	Brighton & HA	D	0-0	0-0		8,387
16		29	H	Scunthorpe U	W	1-1	2-1	Conroy, Freeman	4,566
17	N	2	H	Lincoln C	L	1-1	1-2	Carpenter	6,945
18		9	A	Cardiff C	W	2-0	2-1	Conroy, Blake	6,144
19		19	H	Barnet	W	1-0	2-0	Conroy, Morgan	4,423
20		23	A	Wigan A	D	0-0	1-1	Scott	5,039
21		30	H	Brighton & HA	W	1-0	2-0	Conroy, Blake	8,279
22	D	3	A	Chester C	D	0-0	1-1	Freeman	1,762
23		14	H	Leyton O	D	0-0	1-1	Watson	7,355
24		21	A	Scarborough	W	2-0	2-0	Conroy, Scott	2,015
25		26	H	Exeter C	D	1-1	1-1	Angus	7,892
26	J	11	H	Darlington	W	1-0	6-0	Scott, Carpenter, Cullip, Freeman, Brooker, Conroy	5,735
27		14	A	Colchester U	L	0-1	1-2	Morgan	3,820
28		18	A	Torquay U	L	1-0	1-3	Scott	3,386
29		25	A	Scunthorpe U	W	3-0	4-1	Cusack, Conroy, Blake, Scott	3,259
30		31	H	Cardiff C	L	0-1	1-4	(Eckhardt og)	6,459
31	F	8	A	Lincoln C	L	0-1	0-2		3,948
32		11	H	Swansea C	W	0-0	2-1	Freeman, Brooker	4,836
33		15	H	Wigan A	D	0-0	1-1	Blake	9,448
34		22	A	Barnet	D	1-1	2-2	Conroy, Scott	3,316
35	M	1	H	Chester C	D	0-1	1-1	Morgan	5,780
36		8	H	Scarborough	W	2-0	4-0	Cockerill, Freeman, Blake, Warren	6,080
37		16	A	Leyton O	W	0-0	2-0	Blake, Carpenter	7,125
38		22	H	Hartlepool U	W	1-0	1-0	Freeman	7,222
39		29	A	Hereford U	D	0-0	0-0		4,473
40		31	H	Rochdale	W	1-1	1-1	Conroy	8,766
41	A	5	A	Carlisle U	W	0-0	2-1	Conroy, McAree	9,171
42		8	A	Mansfield T	D	0-0	0-0		3,912
43		12	H	Northampton T	L	0-1	0-1		11,479
44		19	A	Doncaster R	D	0-0	0-0		2,920
45		26	H	Hull C	W	1-0	2-0	Morgan 2	10,588
46	M	3	A	Cambridge U	W	1-0	1-0	Freeman	7,218

	Apps
	Sub
	Goals

			FA CUP					
1	N	16	A	Plymouth A	L	0-1	0-5		7,104
			COCA COLA CUP					
1/1	A	20	A	Southend U	W	1-0	2-0	Conroy, Watson	3,084
2/1	S	3	H	Southend U	L	0-2	1-2	Conroy	4,297
1/2		17	H	Ipswich T	D	1-0	1-1	Morgan	6,947
2/2		24	A	Ipswich T	L	1-1	2-4	Brooker, (Sedgley og)	6,825

Watson	Herrera	Cullip	Cusack	Blake	McAtee	Mison	Conroy	Morgan	Scott	Hamill	Brooker	Thomas	Cockerill	Angus	Freeman	Lange	Adams	Marshall	Carpenter	Davis	Soloman	Parker	Lawrence	Hartfield	Stewart	Warren	
2	3	4	5	6	7	8^	9	10	11"	S	13	14															1
2	3	4*	5	6	7^		9	10	11			12	8	S	14												2
2"	3^	4	5	6	7*		9	10	11			13	8	14	12	1											3
2	3	4	5	6		12	9	10	11"			13	8	S	7*	1											4
2	3	4	5	6	S		9	10	11		S	S		8	7	1											5
2	3	4	5	6	14		9	10	11^		S	S		8	7	1											6
2	3	4^	5	6	S		9	10	11*		12		14	8	7	1											7
2	3	4"	5	6	13		9	10	12		14		8*	11	7^												8
2	3		4	6		12	9*	10	7"		14	13		5	11^				8								9
2	3	S	4	6			9	10	7*		12	13		5	11"				8								10
2	3	14	4	6			9	10	7^		S			5	11		S		8								11
2	3		4	6			9	10	7"		S	S		5	11			13	8								12
2	3		4	6		S	9	10	7"			S		5	11				8	13							13
2	3		4	6		13	9	10	7*		14	12		5"	11^				8								14
2	3	S	4	6			9	10	7^			13	14	5"	11				8								15
2	3	5	4	6	S		9	10	11		S		14		7^				8								16
2	3	5	4	5			9	10	11		S		14	6^	7				8								17
2	3	5	4	6			9	10*	11"		13		8	12	S	1			7								18
2	3	14	4	6			9	10	11		S	12	8*	5		1			7^								19
2	3	9	4	6				10	11		14	S	8^	5		1			7		S						20
2	3	5	4	6			9	10	11				8	5	12	1			7*		S						21
2	3*	S	4	6			9	10	11				8	5	12	1			7		S						22
2	3	14	4	6^			9	10	12			S	8*	5	11	1			7								23
2	12		4	6		14	9	10	11^				8	5	7*	1	3"			13							24
2		S	4	6	S		9	10	11		12		8	5	7	1					3*						25
2	3	6"					9	10	11*		14	13	8^	5	12	1			7				4				26
2*	3	6	14				9	10	11		13		8"	5	12	1			7^				4				27
2"	3*	12	4	6			9	10	11^		13		14	5	7	1			8								28
2		5	4	6		S	9	10	11		S	13	8"		7	1			3								29
	5*	4	6	14			9	10	11		12	13			7	1	3		8^		2"						30
		4*	6^				9	10	11		13	3	8		14				5"				2	7	12		31
3			4	6			9	10	11*		12	2"	8		7				5				13		S		32
3			4	6			9	10	11^		12	2	8*		7				5				S	14			33
3			4	6			9*	10	12		13	2	8^		7"				5				14	11			34
3		S	4	6				10	14		13	2	8"		7^				5				9	11			35
3		12	4	6				10	11		13	14	8^		7"				5				2			9*	36
3		8	4	6		12		10	11*		13	14			7"				5				2			9^	37
3			4	6			14	10	11"		13	12		5	7^				8*				2			9	38
3		S	4	6			14	10	11^		13			5	7"				8				2			9	39
3		S	4	6			9	10	12		13			5	7*				8				2			11"	40
3		6	4		7		9^	10	14		S	12	8	5									2			11*	41
3		6	4		7*		9^	10	14		13	12	8	5									2			11"	42
3		6	4	14			9		7"		13	12	8	5^					10				2*			11	43
3		5	4	6			9				13	11"	8	S	7*				10				2			12	44
3		5	4	6			9	10^				12	8"	14	7*				11				2			13	45
3		5	4	6			9"	10				12	8*	14	7^				11				2			13	46
44	26	23	44	40	5	1	40	44	36	-	-	6	27	28	32	18	2	-	34	-	1	3	13	1	2	8	A
-	-	6	1	1	4	3	3	-	7	-	26	20	5	4	7	-	1	-	1	1	-	2	1	1	1	3	S
3	-	1	2	7	1	-	21	8	9	-	2	-	1	1	9	-	-	-	5	-	-	-	-	-	-	1	G

Watson	Herrera	Cullip	Cusack	Blake	McAtee	Mison	Conroy	Morgan	Scott	Hamill	Brooker	Thomas	Cockerill	Angus	Freeman	Lange	Adams	Marshall	Carpenter	Davis	Soloman	Parker	Lawrence	Hartfield	Stewart	Warren	
2	3	5	4	6			9	10	11			13	S	8"	12		1		7								1
2	3	4	5	6	7	S	9	10	11*			12	8	S													1/1
	3^	4	5	6	S	13	9	10	11			2	8"	14	7	1											1/2
2	3	4*	5	6	S		9	10	12		S		8	11	7												2/1
2"	3	4^	5	6		12	9	10	7			13		11				8*	14								2/2

7.

The Fayed Effect: 1998-99

Background

Winning promotion with Adams in 1997 was the start of something at Fulham that was little short of a revolution. Within weeks, chairman Jimmy Hill had gone, ending an association with the club that stretched back to 1952. Vice-chairman Bill Muddyman found the man who could provide the financial support he felt the club needed to progress. It was the unlikely figure of Mohamed Al Fayed, the controversial owner of Harrods, who became the Cottagers' new owner. A highly successful businessman, his interests stretched beyond retailing but football was a brand new venture for him. Many questioned his motives but no one could doubt his impact.

Every area of the club felt the Fayed effect – and it was unquestionably for the better. Over time, substantial sums of money was spent on the ground, top-class training facilities at Motspur Park were purchased, more attention was paid to marketing the club, and there was a huge investment in new and professional staff. In a remarkably short space of time, Fulham Football Club shook off its old fashioned sleepy image and became a seriously professional club.

There were of course casualties as the club moved out of its comfort zone in an attempt to reclaim its place in the top tier. Jimmy Hill and his co-directors Tom

Wilson and Cyril Swain were the first to go. But if the money spent on the infrastructure was to be justified, there had to be success on the pitch, and it had to happen sooner rather than later. The new chairman was prepared to spend to make it happen and 'consolidation' was not a word in his dictionary. He was impatient for results and he wanted success with style, the type of football that excited crowds and would get Fulham talked about and admired.

So, it became clear early on that Adams, a decent, hardworking but relatively low-profile manager, and many of his thoroughly professional but essentially journeyman players, did not measure up to the demands of the new owner. Within weeks of the start of the 1997-98 season, a new management team arrived at the Cottage and in terms of a glamour appointment, there was little to equal Kevin Keegan. A charismatic figure and one of soccer's best-known names, he had been out of football since leaving Newcastle nine months earlier. Keegan was persuaded to become involved in the lower levels of English football for the first time since leaving Scunthorpe in 1971 and took the rather cumbersome title of Chief Operating Officer. He brought in with him as Team Manager his former England colleague Ray Wilkins.

The two set about transforming Fulham's playing squad, spending money on a scale previously unimaginable at the Cottage. Names like Ian Selly, Paul Peschisolido

The Championship squad at the start of the season. Back row left to right: Chris Smith (physio), Palmer, Neilsen, Trollope, Arnott, Moody, Symons, Mahar, McGuckin, Lawrence, Davis. Middle row: Malcolm Martin (asst physo), Alex Court (physiologist), Peschisolido, Brevett, Selly, Cornwall, Arendse, Taylor, McAree, Morgan, MacAnespie, Uhlenbeek, John Marshall (youth team coach), Alan Bevan (kit manager). Front row: Smith, Scott, Collins, Coleman, Bracewell (player coach), Kevin Keegan (COO), Frank Sibley (asst manager), Brazier, Brooker, Salako, Hayward.

and Chris Coleman arrived in the autumn of 1997 from Premiership clubs at ever-increasing transfer fees. In 1997-98, the transition year between Adams and Keegan (or Hill and Fayed), Fulham used 39 different players in 46 matches, a club record. Of the team that played in the closing games of that season, only Blake, Morgan and Lawrence had played in the promotion side 12 months earlier. The turnover of the squad was breath-taking and Keegan could be forgiven for repeating Tommy Docherty's famous pre-match team talk in the 1970s. After he had bought and sold many players, he allegedly said to his new charges, 'Good luck, whoever you are'.

Not surprisingly, the team did not gel from the start. Results in 1997-98 were inconsistent and performances quite disappointing. In the end, Fulham had to settle for sixth place, scraping into the last Play-off spot on goals scored. But that was as good as it got. Grimsby managed a draw in the first leg at the Cottage and won 1-0 at Blundell Park and so the Fayed master plan was put on hold for a year, but not before yet more changes.

Even before the Play-off games, Keegan had dispensed with Wilkins as team manager, assuming those responsibilities for himself. As his principal lieutenants, he had Frank Sibley as assistant manager, Paul Bracewell as coach and his old Newcastle mentor, Arthur Cox as chief scout. And he continued to tamper with the squad. The most significant additions were defenders Kit Symons from Manchester City and Steve Finnan from Notts County and strikers Geoff Horsfield from Halifax and Barry Hayles from Bristol Rovers. All four featured prominently in 1998-99 and were to prove valuable longer-term acquisitions for the club.

With the squad they had, it was no surprise that Fulham went into the season as promotion favourites. The manager's boast about building a team that could compete at the next level up did not look an idle one. But, even allowing for the usual pre-season hyperbole, few would have predicted the record-breaking season that lay ahead or that come the celebrations in May, Keegan himself would no longer be there.

Straight Down to Business

The campaign began with games against two clubs from the same part of the north west playing at this level for the first time and both destined to leave the division but in different directions at the end of the season. Macclesfield's modest Moss Rose ground in front of a crowd of 3,933 was the unlikely starting point for Fulham's record breaking season. It took just 19 minutes for the Cottagers to give notice of their intentions to the other 23 clubs in the division. Trollope was fouled 25 yards

Kevin Keegan in the dugout.

Dirk Lehmann on the mark in the opening home game against Manchester City.

from goal and Bracewell slipped the ball to former Palace and England player John Salako whose shot was wide of the wall and beyond the goalkeeper. It was the only goal of an open game in which Fulham's new German striker, Dirk Lehmann, might have had a hat-trick. From one of the smallest clubs in the third tier to the biggest as the Cottagers began their home fixtures in a televised game against newly-relegated Manchester City on a Friday evening. The fallen giants of English football were playing outside the top two divisions for the first time and, despite City's status as promotion favourites, Fulham emerged convincing 3-0 winners. It was all over as a contest by half-time. Fulham scored their three goals in the space of 25 first half minutes, through Beardsley and then two from Lehmann.

Beating Colchester 1-0 at Layer Road a week later made it three wins out of three and no goals conceded. In a game in which defences had the upper hand, Fulham got the only goal eight minutes from time when Collins was on hand to hammer Peschisolido's cross into the net. Colchester did get the ball in the net but it was disallowed for offside.

A couple of draws slowed Fulham's progress and made them aware that they would have to work hard against opponents who could match them for effort if not ability. Bournemouth went to the Cottage with a 100 per cent record from their three games but seemed content to shut up shop and claim a point. A fierce long-range Morgan drive that rattled a post was the closest either side came to scoring. Just 48 hours later, on Bank Holiday Monday, the Cottagers were on the road again, to Oldham. Fulham had lost on their last five visits to Boundary Park but came close to ending the run. A Moody header put the visitors ahead five minutes after the interval but Oldham equalised with a goal the Fulham defence was convinced was offside. The referee said it was not and so they conceded their first goal after 422 minutes of the season and dropped two more points. Still, 11 points out of 15 and second place in the table as not a bad return on the month.

A Rhythm Emerges

As summer gave way to autumn, so Fulham found their rhythm and started to accumulate points. A busy September, which included two Worthington Cup ties against Premiership Southampton, yielded 10 points from five games. October was more rewarding with nine from 12, helping to keep Keegan's men in the promotion frame. That month also saw the arrival of a new striker, Geoff Horsfield, from Halifax for a bargain £325,000. He scored on his debut and his all-action no-nonsense style made him an immediate terrace favourite. Despite not starting with Fulham until the 13th game, Horsfield was to finish the season as the club's top scorer. It was Lehmann who made way for him. He, too, was popular with the supporters but he was an unlucky striker. Goalkeepers saved their best for his shots and he seemed to hit the woodwork more often than anyone else. But two goals in one game was not the sort of return Keegan was looking for from his main striker.

September was supposed to start with a home game against Wycombe but it was postponed because of Fulham's international call ups, something that was not a common occurrence in the third tier. The month started against Stoke instead. Relegated the previous May but revitalised under new manager Brian Little, the Potters had taken maximum points from their first six games and this First v Second clash drew 12,055 for a Tuesday evening kick-off. The game started badly for Fulham, especially for front man Moody who fell awkwardly and sustained an injury that kept him out until the final weeks of the season. A tightly fought game was settled on the hour. After playing a neat one-two with Bracewell, full-back Brevett found himself in the clear on the left hand side of the penalty area. He shot across the goal to score for the only time in his 175 League games for the Cottagers.

There followed two disappointing performances and results. Against a Notts County side that had yet to win at home, Fulham lost for the first time. The Magpies scored just before the interval, Murray heading in from 12 yards, but they owed the three points to an outstanding performance by goalkeeper Ward. If losing at

Against Stoke in September, Brevett got the winner and his only League goal for Fulham.

Meadow Lane was unlucky, drawing at home with York was careless. The Cottagers scored three times but failed to win against a team destined to be relegated. Debutant Luke Cornwall put the Cottagers ahead after 19 minutes, a lead they held for 10 minutes until Agnew equalised. And this set the pattern for the game. Coleman headed Fulham into a half-time lead but Tolson equalised early in the second half, again with a header. York had a player sent off and the Cottagers took advantage through Symons. But the visitors equalised for a third time through Agnew with five minutes remaining and for all their pressure, Keegan's men could not regain the advantage. A very disappointing result and clearly two points dropped.

This was almost the last time that season Fulham were as generous. After the York draw, they won eight of the next nine matches and soared up the table. There were also two more signing in November, defender Steve Finnan from Notts County and striker Barry Hayles from Bristol Rovers. Yet again, Keegan had spent the money wisely. Although they took time to settle, both Finnan and Hayles were to serve the club well for several seasons, and at the highest level. All the pieces were now in place and the Cottagers push for promotion gathered momentum.

Cup Adventures

For most teams concentrating on promotion, Cup competitions can be a distraction but for Keegan they were a chance to test his players against clubs from the top two divisions. He had claimed that most of his purchases were made with at least one eye on the following seasons when he expected Fulham to be playing at a higher level. This view was amply rewarded by the Cottagers' progress in both domestic Cup competitions which took them to the biggest clubs in the country where they performed with great credit.

In the early weeks of the season, Third Division Cardiff were eliminated from the Worthington Cup, Fulham winning both legs 2-1. Then a major shock. Premiership Southampton were not only held to a 1-1 draw on their own ground but were beaten in the second leg at the Cottage by a Lehmann goal. The prize was a third round trip to Anfield, which is where the journey ended. The match was played in pouring rain and televised live on Sky. After going a goal down in the 54th minute when Thompson's long range shot took a huge deflection, the Cottagers equalised with a wonderful Peschisolido strike. He curled a brilliant shot from the edge of the box into the roof of the net which gave goalkeeper Freidel no chance. But the Reds proved too strong and scored twice in the last 25 minutes. Fulham lost but they gave Liverpool a harder time than several Premiership clubs would that season.

Non-League Leigh RMI were the first opponents in the FA Cup and, after a sensational display by the visitors' goalkeeper Felgate at the Cottage, Fulham needed a replay to progress to round two. This was another home draw, to Hartlepool from Division Three, who impressed with their neat, thoughtful football. The 4-2 scoreline was harsh on the visitors. It was not until the last 10 minutes that Keegan's men got the two goals that settled the tie, through Morgan and Horsfield, but they were now through to join the big clubs.

Just as in the Worthington Cup, Fulham were paired with Premiership Southampton and just as in the Worthington Cup, they drew 1-1 at the Dell and won 1-0 at the Cottage, so it was in the FA Cup. At the Dell, a Hayward goal earned a replay and at the Cottage, a Hayles goal secured a fourth round trip to League leaders Aston Villa. It was the first FA Cup meeting between the clubs since Fulham's non-League days of 1905 and the first time for 16 years that the Cottagers had made it through to the last 32. Despite their lofty League position, all was not well behind the scenes at Villa Park and Fulham took full advantage. Hayward and Morgan, both from Villa-supporting Midlands families, scored in the first half. The Cottagers held on surprisingly comfortably in the second to pull off a sensational but thoroughly deserved win.

Not since the Cup Final year of 1975 had Fulham had last played in the fifth round, or played four ties against clubs from a higher level in a single season. In 1999 the fourth was treble-chasing Manchester United at Old Trafford. The match was televised live on a Sunday afternoon and 8,500 Fulham fans took up the club's full allocation of tickets, many travelling on the train service heavily subsidised by the chairman. The Cottagers were without four key players, Bracewell, Morgan and Peschisolido all injured and Horsfield who was suspended, but they still gave United a scare. The only goal came on 25 minutes from Cole, a Fulham old boy Keegan had sold to United when he was Newcastle manager. Far from being cowed, the visitors fought back and were a Salako toenail away from an equaliser but could not force a replay.

Back to Business

So the Cup runs ended. For Fulham they had been exciting, profitable and educational but the real business was getting out of the Second Division. And despite the high-profile Worthington and FA Cup ties, they were not deflected from their principal objective. The only points dropped between the end of September and the end of November were in a strange game at home to Luton. In a lacklustre performance, the Cottagers were three goals down to a mid-table Hatters side, all headers, before they got going. All they could manage in reply was a late consolation headed goal from Alan Neilson. Since this defeat (which was to prove the last home defeat of the season) came on the back of two impressive victories, it was even harder to understand. The previous week, the Cottagers had gone to Lincoln, something of a bogey ground in the past, and won 2-0, thanks to two Beardsley goals. The first was controversial, awarded when the referee penalised the Lincoln goalkeeper for handling a back pass when a Fulham player appeared to be the last one to touch the ball. Somehow, with nine Lincoln players on the goal line, Beardsley managed to squeeze the ball in. At home in midweek, bottom-of-the-table Wycombe were comfortably beaten with goals from Coleman and Bracewell. Wanderers' task was made even harder when defender Wright was sent off with the score at 1-0.

Bouncing back after the Luton defeat was essential and there are few less welcoming venues for visiting teams than Millwall's Den. It was clearly a big test, made marginally easier by the dismissal of the Lions' full-back Stuart for two fouls within 90 seconds. Despite dominating possession, the Cottagers had to wait until the 87th minute to score the decisive goal, Symons heading in Hayward's angled cross. It was a hard-earned but vital three points which set Fulham up for a run of five wins on the trot. By the time the run ended, Fulham topped the table two points better off than Stoke with a game in hand and three new players, Horsfield, Finnan and Hayles, signed and in the team.

After Millwall came promotion rivals Walsall at the Cottage and in torrential rain and a strong wind, Fulham demolished the Saddlers 4-1, a satisfactory afternoon rounded off with a goal for new boy Horsfield. He was on the mark again a week later when the Cottagers went to Blackpool and notched up their fifth away win in seven League games. In the Seasiders' line up was Micky Conroy, who had been a star in Fulham's promotion side two seasons earlier but such was the recent turnover at the Cottage that Morgan was the only one of his former colleagues still in the side. And it was Morgan who opened the scoring on 24 minutes. There were three more goals in the next 12 minutes, two for Fulham (a Hayward penalty and a Peschisolido shot from 12 yards). Although Blackpool pulled it back to 3-2 with 25 minutes remaining, the Cottagers held on for maximum points.

November started with nine points from three games, the first a home win over Bristol Rovers. Although Fulham dominated territorially, it took a scrambled 36th minute goal by Collins to settle the issue. Only 3,485 were at a dilapidated Racecourse Ground in midweek to see the Cottagers sew up a match against a Wrexham side that included Ian Rush by half-time. After Hayward had missed a penalty, Dutch-

Peschisolido opens the scoring against Walsall in October.

man Gus Uhlenbeek broke the deadlock on 14 minutes from Peschisolido's cross and the Canadian himself settled the issue on the half hour following up Lehmann's shot which had been parried. Both Finnan and Hayles made their Fulham debuts against Chesterfield at home, a game settled by two Peschisolido goals, one in each half. The first was a spectacular 25-yard shot and the second was a penalty after Horsfield had been brought down. Even though Chesterfield doubled their away goals total for the season in the 55th minute when Howard scored from close range, it was not enough. Fulham held on to win 2-1.

Any thoughts of an easy stroll to promotion after this winning sequence quickly evaporated in a three-day spell at the end of November. Gillingham's Priestfield Stadium has never been a happy hunting ground for Fulham and in November 1998, the Gills were unbeaten in 12 games and in sixth place when the Cottagers made the short journey to Kent. They returned empty handed after a bruising encounter. In a match of very few chances, Gillingham got the only goal, deep into added time when Taylor got his head to a cross by Hodge. The following Tuesday, Fulham suffered back-to-back defeats for the only time that season. It was at Wigan that Keegan's Fulham career had started 14 months earlier (with a 2-1 defeat) and it was Wigan who pipped Micky Adams' team to the Third Division title in 1997. The jinx continued in 1998 and two goals in 10 second half minutes, from McGibbon and Lowe, were Fulham's undoing. A great chance to get back in the game was squandered after 64 minutes when Hayward again missed a penalty after Finnan had been upended. Even when Fulham got the ball in the net through Horsfield, it was adjudged offside.

Top Spot Claimed and Held

Very briefly, Keegan's team slipped out of the promotion places, but it proved to be only temporary. There were still 27 games to go and, remarkably, Fulham were to lose only three of them, one after promotion and the title had been won. It was the week before Christmas, following a win at Preston, that they went top of the table for the first time, and once there, never faltered. The consistency was remarkable. There were 15 clean sheets in the 27 games and 13 different goalscorers, and promotion was sewn up with a month of the season (and six games) to go. At the end of January, Fulham had a three point lead at the top over Preston and a game in hand. By the end of February, the lead had stretched to six points (still over Preston) and a game in hand. At the end of March, Walsall were the nearest challengers, but the gap was 13 points from the same number of games. In the winter of 1999, the Cottagers were remorselessly successful.

Burnley (at home 4-0), Preston (away 1-0) and Colchester (home 2-0) were all beaten before the turn of the year without conceding a goal and the seven goals were scored by six different players. Morgan, in his 350th game for Fulham, scored twice in the comfortable victory over Burnley, which was Fulham's best of the season. Preston, one of six clubs the Cottagers have met in every level of the League, made Fulham work much harder, as might be expected from a side managed by David Moyes and which had only been beaten three times that season. The game was fought out largely in midfield until the decisive moment in the 82nd minute when Coleman got his head to a Hayles chip to nod in the winner. A midday kick-off at home on Boxing Day drew a crowd of 12,436 who saw the Cottagers complete the first of nine 'doubles' that season, over Colchester. Fulham led 1-0 through Smith's first half goal when Colchester goalkeeper Emberson was sent off for bringing down Lehmann. Hayles converted the penalty and sealed the win. Emberson's dismissal was the seventh red card in the previous eight games between the clubs and in only two of the games had both sides finished with a full complement of players.

A draw at Northampton marked the halfway stage of the season and the end of 1998. The Cobblers were draw specialists, having shared the points in six of their 10 previous home games. It was only after Horsfield had given Fulham the lead five minutes into the second half that the home side became attack minded and with 20 minutes to go, Freestone equalised. Just as Fulham faced Macclesfield in the opening game of the season, so the Cheshire club provided the opposition for the first game of 1999. And the score was the same at the Cottage as it was at Moss Rose, a 1-0 win for Fulham. It was a sluggish display by the Cottagers on a rain-soaked pitch against the relegation strugglers and they were grateful for Horsfield's fortunate second half deflection to win the match.

The last major setback for Fulham before clinching promotion was a big defeat at Maine Road to an in-form Manchester City who were starting to make a push for promotion. Played at a furious pace, there were many robust challenges which the referee viewed benignly. City were 3-0 up after 54 minutes, exactly reversing the scoreline at the Cottage, and the game was over. As Keegan admitted afterwards, 'They had a bit more commitment than us on the day'.

After that, it was plain sailing. An unbeaten run of 15 matches, all but two of which were won, ensured that the victory over Gillingham in April secured one of the two promotion places. It needed one more win after that to guarantee the title and that came in the next home match against Millwall. Fulham were having to cope with teams intent more on defending than winning and hoping for a point and some of the narrow scorelines did not reflect the extent to which the Cottagers dominated play. Home victories over Oldham (1-0) and Northampton (2-0) in January were good examples. Keegan did add to the squad that month, a loan signing of a player he worked with at Newcastle. Philip Albert came into the midfield when Bracewell was injured and oozed class from the first.

From February's four League games, Fulham took 10 points, a draw at Wycombe (in Lawrie Sanchez's first game in charge of Wanderers) the only game they failed to win. Horsfield was now making his mark with five goals in the next three games played over eight days against Notts County (home 2-1), Reading (home 3-1) and

Symons (light shirt, centre) scores the winner at Bournemouth in March, one of his 11 goals from central defence.

York (away 3-0). There was also an increasing and important goalscoring contribution from central-defender Symons. He had scored Fulham's goal at Wycombe in the 1-1 draw and the third against Reading. The following month, the Welsh international was on the mark at Dean Court as the Cottagers drew for the second time with Bournemouth (the only club they did not beat at least once during the season), the opening goal in a thrilling 3-2 Friday evening win in the pouring rain at Bristol Rovers (where the winner was scored by future Rovers manager Trollope), the only goal of a vital Tuesday evening game at Stoke and one of the four in the 4-0 home thrashing of Blackpool.

Symons also scored one of the two goals which accounted for Wigan at the Cottage early in April, Albert getting the other. This came days after a Morgan goal had seen off Reading at the Madejski Stadium, a win which equalled the club record of 12 away wins and 87 points in a season. Wigan arrived at the Cottage having just qualified for a Wembley Final (the Auto Windscreens) and on a run that had taken them to the fringes of the Play-offs. But all of that was overshadowed by a visit to the Cottage of singer Michael Jackson whose appearance alongside chairman Fayed generated a lot of excitement among sections of the 12,140 crowd. But the points won that day, plus the fact that Walsall and Preston both lost, meant that only three more points were needed to reclaim the place in the second tier of the League that the Cottagers had lost in 1986.

Lows and Highs in the Home Straight

While the players were getting on with collecting the points, there was a massive upset behind the scenes. Early in February, the FA had terminated Glenn Hoddle's contract as England coach for inappropriate remarks he had made about disabled people. Howard Wilkinson took over on a caretaker basis but was not seen as the long-term successor. Although he was only managing in the third tier, Keegan seemed to be the choice of the media pundits who clamoured for his appointment. His stance was evasive, sometimes saying he wanted the job, sometimes claiming he could do both and at others saying he was happy at Fulham. The uncertainty and on-going speculation were very unhelpful but what upset Fulham supporters most was the manager's lack of candour. Nobody would have blamed him for wanting to manage his country but it was his unwillingness to commit to either England or Fulham that was so annoying. And when he announced on television his intention to take the England job, it seemed a shabby way to treat Mohamed Al Fayed, his players and staff at the Cottage and the club's supporters.

Keegan's initial response was to say yes to the England job in March, but only for four games. He remained at the Cottage and was in the dugout for the Tuesday evening visit of Gillingham, which attracted an above-average crowd of 13,119. It took Fulham 22 minutes to make the breakthrough. Horsfield picked up a loose ball and as the defenders converged on him, slipped it to an unmarked Hayles who applied the finishing touch. The Gills did not let Fulham have it all their own way. Their defence was tight and they pushed for an equaliser but it was Fulham who got the next vital goal. It came in the 79th minute and was very soft. Coleman back-heeled a Hayward corner and with goalkeeper and defenders leaving it for each other, the ball trickled into the net. With four minutes remaining, Brevett burst into the box and was brought down. Hayward and Hayles between them had missed Fulham's previous three penalties and this time Horsfield stepped up and scored at the second attempt after his first shot had been parried.

A powerful Horsfield header wins the home match against Lincoln.

The first and most important part of the job had been completed, with promotion secured after 40 of the 46 games. Part two was to take the divisional title and supporters did not have long to wait to see the Cottagers claim only their third piece of silverware in 81 seasons of League football. They might have done it at Saltergate but for only the sixth time that season, Fulham were beaten. Chesterfield scored the only goal of the game in the 77th minute through Hewitt and the Spireites probably deserved the three points on the day.

In a Friday evening thriller, Symons opens the scoring against Bristol Rovers.

A typical Symons header, and the winner at Stoke in March.

A week after clinching promotion the Cottagers finally took the Second Division title. Walsall's defeat the previous evening ensured the title was destined for SW6 before a ball was kicked but the supporters wanted to see Fulham win it in their own right and not by default. Mid-table Millwall, who had reached the Auto Wind-screens Final, were the visitors to the Cottage for a re-arranged midweek fixture. There was little the south London club could do to stop Fulham's coronation once Kevin Betsy, deputising for the suspended Horsfield, had given them the lead after 20 minutes. Hayles made it 2-0 before the break and then another Symons header, his 11th goal of the season and the second against Millwall, made it 3-0 within five minutes of the re-start. This was the cue for the Lions best spell and although Shaw reduced the arrears, Finnan restored the three-goal advantage in the final minute. It was a convincing and appropriate victory in front of 11,266 jubilant supporters and the first important step in the Fayed plan to take Fulham back to the highest level.

There were four matches remaining but, with the target achieved, there was a sense of anti-climax. A home game against a defence-minded Wrexham was drawn, as was an away game at Walsall, the team that had clinched second place in the table. In between was a 1-0 defeat at Burnley, a petulant and acrimonious encounter in which Fulham lost four players to injury and had Symons sent off. He was shown a second yellow card after a 90th minute clash in which many people thought he was the innocent party. It was the Cottagers first dismissal of the season but they still had one of the best disciplinary records in the division. Only three clubs managed fewer than their 52 bookings but they all had more sendings off while only Blackpool had no dismissals but accumulated 87 yellow cards.

The curtain came down on a memorable season with a home game against Preston and it was party time. Fulham cantered to a 3-0 win thanks to a hat-trick in

Betsy scores the first goal in the Championship clincher against Millwall in April.

The first paypack on the chairman's investment.

A rare Finnan goal, at home against Blackpool in March.

Celebrating the season.

13 second half minutes by substitute Moody in his final appearance for the club. It was the only Fulham treble of the season and comprised a fierce shot, a penalty and a header, a wonderful way to sign off before the season's-best attendance of 17,176. After the match, the club was presented with the Second Division trophy, 50 years and a day after they had last won it. There were several members of the 1948-49 side in the crowd as guests of the club who saw a spectacular ceremony with all the players and the staff involved in the carefully orchestrated celebrations. The only dampener on the occasion was that 48 hours earlier, Keegan had announced on television that he was leaving the Cottage to take on the England job full time, a decision he was not the only one to regret in the fullness of time.

Reflections

It was 50 years and one day after winning their first piece of silverware that Fulham were presented with their second. Just as in 1949 it was the Second Division Championship, so again in 1999 it was the Division Two trophy, though this time it was in reality the third tier of the League. For all the money that had been spent on assembling the team, the manner of the success was still remarkable. The team set or equalled 13 club records playing the sort of football the chairman expected. And the public responded. For the first time since 1982-83, Fulham's average attendance was in five figures (11,409), and was the fourth highest since they dropped out of the top flight in 1968.

A total of 31 players was used in the League, including Jamie Smith who came on loan from Palace for the last nine matches. The nucleus of the side comprised Taylor in goal, full-back Brevett, defenders Symons and Coleman and midfield player Hayward, all of whom played in at least 40 of the 46 games. Morgan, Smith, Brace-well, Horsfield and Hayles played in at least half the matches. Morgan, Lawrence (1 appearance), Brooker (I substitute outing) and Scott (2+1 matches) were the only survivors of the Adams promotion squad of two years earlier. Both Hayward and Moody (2+5 games), however, were both signed by Adams in the 1997 close season and Davis (15) was already at the Cottage when Keegan arrived. This meant that 24 of the 31 players used to win the title had been signed by Keegan and the other 23 players used by his predecessor to win promotion just 24 months earlier had all left the club.

The club records set in that memorable season are worth listing because they show the all-round strength of the team.

Most points in a season (101) even after converting all the others to three points for a win. The previous best was 87 in 1958-59 and 1996-97.

Most home points in a season (60), five more than in 1958-59.

Most home wins (19) compared with the old record of 18 in 1958-59.

Consecutive home wins (15). The previous best was 12.

Fewest home defeats (1), which equalled 1912-13 and 1948-49 when fewer games were played.

Most away wins (12) equalled the Micky Adams' team record in 1996-97.

Most home and away doubles (9), one more than in 1931-32.

Most wins in a season (31), four more than in 1958-59).

Fewest defeats (7) two less than in 1931-32, 1948-49, 1958-59 and 1996-97.

Most consecutive wins (8) compared with the previous best of 7 in 1958.

Most clean sheets (24). Up to then, the best was 20 in 1996-97.

Most individual scorers (23). In 1907-08 and 1996-97, the number was 17.

The 32 goals conceded (over 46 games) equalled the previous best defensive record set in 1922-23 when only 42 games were played.

Never before had a Fulham side swept all before it to such an extent but as they celebrated at Harrods in May 1999, the hierarchy must have wondered who could succeed Keegan and what could he do for an encore. Was the Cottagers surge through the divisions to continue or would it peak in the division where they had spent 48 of their 80 seasons as a League club?

Summary Statistics

End	Played	Points	Position
September	10	21	5
October	14	30	2
November	18	39	3
December	23	49	1
January	27	58	1
February	31	68	1
March	37	84	1
April	43	97	1
Final	**46**	**101**	**1**

	H	A	Total
P	23	23	**46**
W	19	12	**31**
D	3	5	**8**
L	1	6	**7**
F	50	29	**79**
A	12	20	**32**
Pts	60	41	**101**

0 points v	*1 point v*	*2 points v*	*3 points v*	*4 points v*	*6 points v*
		Bournemouth	Burnley	North'pton T	Blackpool
			Chesterfield	Oldham A	Bristol R
			Gillingham	Walsall	Colchester U
			Luton T	Wrexham	Lincoln C
			Man C	Wycombe W	Macclesfield T
			Notts C	York C	Millwall
			Wigan A		Preston NE
					Reading
					Stoke C
0 points	**0 points**	**2 points**	**21 points**	**24 points**	**54 points**

The Championship Squad: 1998-99

Maik Taylor: An early Keegan signing from Southampton, Taylor was a former soldier who was a reliable and consistent goalkeeper in 228 games over six seasons at the Cottage. An ever-present in this Championship season, he set a new club record for the number of clean sheets, 24 in 46 League games and four more in Cup games. A Northern Ireland international, he moved to Birmingham in 2003.

Steve Finnan: This classy defender was snapped up for a modest fee from Notts County in November 1998 and in five seasons at the club made 202 appearances and established himself in the Republic of Ireland team. Finnan made the transition from the third to the first tier of the League with Fulham and looked comfortable in the best company. He was transferred to Liverpool in 2003 and played in two Champions League Finals.

Rufus Brevett: Signed by Keegan from QPR the previous season after seven seasons at Loftus Road, Brevett missed only one game in 1998-99 and his whole-hearted displays at left-back made him a crowd favourite. Uncompromising and total committed, he spent six seasons at the Cottage playing 205 times and was great value for the £375,000 fee.

Simon Morgan: The only survivor of Micky Adams' promotion side, Morgan, Fulham's Player of the 1990s (the only one to have played in every season in the decade), was equally at home in the back four or midfield. Although injuries were starting to take their toll, 36 of his 408 Fulham appearances came in this Championship season. Immensely popular with the Fulham supporters, Morgan had cost just £100,000 from Leicester in 1990.

Kit Symons: A star central-defender at Portsmouth in the early 1990s, Symons had found the going tougher when he moved to Manchester City in 1995. He was snapped up by Keegan on a free transfer and was an immediate success in the back alongside fellow Welsh international Coleman. He also scored 11 goals, several of them match winners, from open play in the Championship season. Symons made 130 appearances for Fulham and is now part of the club's management team as well as working on a part-time basis with Coleman for the Welsh national side.

Chris Coleman: A natural captain and leader, Coleman became an influential figure at the Cottage after his high-profile move in November 1997 from Blackburn for £1.9 million, then a club record. He missed just one game in the Championship season and had an outstanding season. He was part of the First Division Championship side two years later until a serious car crash in January 2001 ended his career. He later managed Fulham (2003-07) and is currently manager of the Welsh national side.

Steve Hayward: Hayward had an terrific season in midfield the year Fulham won promotion with Micky Adams – but for Carlisle, who were also promoted. He signed for Fulham in June 1997, one of Adams' last deals, and he survived the transition to Keegan and played in all but four of the League games in 1998-99. A creative midfield player who was an excellent crosser and dead ball kicker, Hayward played 146 times for Fulham before moving on to Barnsley.

Paul Bracewell: A very experienced midfield player at the highest level, with Stoke, Everton, Sunderland, Newcastle (where Keegan was manager) and England, Bracewell was Keegan's first signing, in October 1997. Despite a string of serious injuries, he had won a cupboard full of League and Cup honours. As well as playing in 26 of the League games in the promotion season, Bracewell was also part of the coaching team, which made him ideally placed when his mentor moved on to the England job. Bracewell, however, had an unhappy time as the club's manager.

Geoff Horsfield: To bolster his attacking options, Keegan paid Halifax just £325,000 for Horsfield in the early weeks of the Championship season. A former miner who had all the attributes of an old fashioned British centre-forward, Horsfield slotted in immediately and scored 15 goals in 26 starts in his first season. Strong and powerful, his running terrified defenders and the Fulham crowd loved him. He only stayed two seasons (74 games and 31 goals) before continuing his nomadic career with Birmingham in 2000.

Paul Peschisolido: This Canadian international striker became Fulham's first £1 million signing when Keegan paid a seven-figure fee to West Brom in October 1997. It was his fourth move since coming to the UK in 1992, and there were several more after Fulham. On the small side for a striker (5ft 6in), he started well at the Cottage but found it hard to sustain. He scored 30 goals in 115 games before he was sold to Sheffield in 2001 after loan spells at QPR and Norwich.

1998-99

League Division Two   *Manager: Kevin Keegan*

No		Date	V	Opponents	R	H-T	F-T	Scorers	Attend	Taylor	Lawrence	Brevett	Symons	Coleman
1	A	8	A	Macclesfield T	W	1-0	1-0	Salako	3,933	1	2	3	4	5
2		14	H	Manchester C	W	3-0	3-0	Lehmann 2, Beardsley	14,284	1		3	6	5
3		22	A	Colchester U	W	0-0	1-0	Collins	6,377	1		3	6	5
4		29	H	Bournemouth	D	0-0	0-0		12,107	1		3	6	5
5		31	A	Oldham A	D	0-0	1-1	Moody	4,744	1		3	6	5
6	S	8	H	Stoke C	W	0-0	1-0	Brevitt	12,055	1		3	6	5
7		12	A	Notts C	L	0-1	0-1		5,805	1		3	6	5
8		19	H	York C	D	2-1	3-3	Cornwall, Coleman, Symons	9,071	1		3	6	5
9		26	A	Lincoln C	W	0-0	2-1	Beardsley 2	4,731	1		3	6	5
10		29	H	Wycombe W	W	1-0	2-0	Coleman, Bracewell	7,447	1		3	6	5
11	O	3	H	Luton T	L	0-1	1-3	Neilson	11,861	1		3	6	5
12		17	A	Millwall	W	0-0	1-0	Symons	11,876	1		3	6	5
13		24	H	Walsall	W	1-0	4-1	Peschisolido, Symons, Hayward, Horsfield	8,452	1		3	6	5
14		31	A	Blackpool	W	3-1	3-2	Morgan, Hayward, Horsfield	5,904	1		3	6	5
15	N	7	H	Bristol R	W	1-0	1-0	Collins	11,575	1		3	6	5
16		10	A	Wrexham	W	2-0	2-0	Uhlenbeek, Peschisolido	3,485	1		3	6	5
17		21	H	Chesterfield	W	1-0	2-1	Peschisolido 2	10,005	1		3	6	5
18		28	A	Gillingham	L	0-0	0-1		7,614	1		3	6	5
19	D	1	A	Wigan A	L	0-0	0-2		3,951	1		3	6	5
20		12	H	Burnley	W	2-0	4-0	Morgan 2, Hayles, Peschisolido	9,987	1		3	6	5
21		19	A	Preston NE	W	0-0	1-0	Coleman	12,321	1		3	6	5
22		26	H	Colchester U	W	1-0	2-0	Smith, Hayles	12,436	1		3	6	5
23		28	A	Northampton T	D	0-0	1-1	Horsfield	7,315	1		3	6	5
24	J	9	H	Macclesfied T	W	0-0	1-0	Horsfield	10,153	1		3	6	5
25		16	A	Manchester C	L	0-2	0-3		30,251	1		3	6	5
26		26	H	Oldham A	W	1-0	1-0	Morgan	8,160	1		3	6	5
27		30	H	Northampton T	W	1-0	2-0	Hayles, Albert	11,641	1		3		5
28	F	6	A	Wycombe W	D	1-1	1-1	Symons	7,538	1		3	6	5
29		20	H	Notts C	W	1-0	2-1	Horsfield 2	11,909	1		3	6	
30		23	H	Reading	W	0-1	3-1	Horsfield 2, Symons	11,247	1		3	6	5
31		27	A	York C	W	2-0	3-0	Horsfield, Hayles, Peschisolido	6,169	1		3	6	5
32	M	2	A	Bournemouth	D	0-0	1-1	Symons	9,928	1		3	6	5
33		6	H	Lincoln C	W	1-0	1-0	Horsfield	11,702	1		3	6	5
34		9	A	Luton T	W	1-0	4-0	Horsfield 2, Trollope, Hayles	7,424	1		3	6	5
35		12	A	Bristol R	W	2-1	3-2	Symons, Horsfield, Trollope	8,011	1		3	6	5
36		16	A	Stoke C	W	1-0	1-0	Symons	12,298	1		3	6	5
37		20	H	Blackpool	W	1-0	4-0	Hayles, Horsfield, Finnan, Symons	12,869	1		3	6	5
38	A	5	A	Reading	W	0-0	1-0	Morgan	18,741	1			6	5
39		10	A	Wigan A	W	0-0	2-0	Albert, Symons	12,140	1		3	6*	5
40		13	H	Gillingham	W	1-0	3-0	Hayles, Coleman, Horsfield	13,119	1		3	6	5
41		17	A	Chesterfield	L	0-1	0-1		5,800	1		3	6	5
42		21	H	Millwall	W	2-0	4-1	Betsy, Hayles, Symons, Finnan	11,266	1		3	6	5
43		24	H	Wrexham	D	1-1	1-1	Peschisolido	11,754	1		3	6	5
44	M	1	A	Burnley	L	0-0	0-1		13,086	1		3	6	5
45		4	A	Walsall	D	1-1	2-2	Smith (J), Hayward	8,326	1		3	6	5
46		8	H	Preston NE	W	0-0	3-0	Moody 3	17,176	1		3	6	5

								Apps	46	1	45	45	45
								Sub	-	-	-	-	-
								Goals	-	-	1	11	4

FA Cup

No		Date	V	Opponents	R	H-T	F-T	Scorers	Attend	Taylor	Lawrence	Brevett	Symons	Coleman
1	N	15	H	Leigh RMI	D	1-1	1-1	Lehmann	7,965	1		3	6	5
R		24	A	Leigh RMI	W	2-0	2-0	Peschisolido 2	7,500	1		3	6	5
2	D	5	H	Hartlepool U	W	1-1	4-2	Horsfield 2, (Di Lella og), Morgan	6,358	1		5	6	5
3	J	2	A	Southampton	D	1-0	1-1	Hayward	12,549	1		3	6	5
R		13	H	Southampton	W	0-0	1-0	Hayles	17,448	1			6	5
4		23	A	Aston Villa	W	2-0	2-0	Morgan Hayward	35,260	1		3	6	5
5	F	14	A	Manchester U	L	0-1	0-1		54,798	1		3	6	5

Worthington Cup

No		Date	V	Opponents	R	H-T	F-T	Scorers	Attend	Taylor	Lawrence	Brevett	Symons	Coleman
1/1	A	11	H	Cardiff C	W	1-1	2-1	Beardsley, Lehmann	4,305			3	6	5
2/2		18	A	Cardiff C	W	2-0	2-1	Salako, Morgan	4,768			3	6	5
2/1	S	15	H	Southampton	D	0-0	1-1	Coleman	9,623			3	6	5
2/2		23	A	Southampton	W	1-0	1-0	Lehmann	11,645			3	6	5
3	O	27	A	Liverpool	L	0-0	1-3	Peschisoldo	22,296			3	6	5

	Bracewell	Lehmann	Collins	Salako	Neilson	Hayward	Beardsley	Brown	Uhlenbbek	Moody	Peschisolido	Arendse	Davis	Cornwall	Brooker	Scott	Smith (N)	Horsfield	Finnan	Hayles	Keller	Brazier	Albert	Betsy	McAnespie	Smith (J)	
	8	9	10	11	S	S	S																				1
	8	9"	10	11*	S	4	7		12	14																	2
	8	9"	12	11*		10	7^		2	14	13																3
	8	9"	2	11^		10	7	S		14	13																4
	8		2	11"	S	10	7	S		9	14																5
	8	14	2*	11^		10	7		12	9"			13														6
	8^	9	11		S	10	7"		2				13	14													7
	8	9	2		S	10	7*		12						11"	14											8
	8	9"	10		S	11	7		2							14											9
	8		2	13		11	7		12			10*		14		9"											10
	8^	10"	2		4	11	7		12				13	14		9*											11
	8	9	4*			11	7		12		10				S		S										12
	8*	9	7			11	S		2		10"						12	14									13
	8	14	7			11	S		2		10						S	9"									14
	8*	9"	7	14		11	13		2		10^						12										15
	8*	9	7	S		11			2		10						12										16
	8"					11	S		12		10						14	9	2	7*							17
						S	S		S		10						8	9	2	7							18
	8"					11	14		12		10*							9	2^	7							19
			14			7			2		10						8*	9"		11	12						20
	8*	S				7			2		10"						11	9	12	14							21
	8*	13				7			2		10"						11	9^		14							22
	8	S				7			2		10"						11	9		14							23
	8	14	S	13	2	4					10							9"	7	11^							24
	8*	9"			2	4					13						12	14	7	11		10^					25
		S	13						12		10*						7	9	2	11			8				26
	8	14	4								13						7	9"	2	11^	S		6				27
	8	14	12			7					10^							9	2	13			4*				28
		14	8^			10			S								4	9	2	11"			5	13			29
		14				7					10*						4	9"	2	11^			8	13			30
						7					14						4	9"	2	11^		12	8*	13			31
		9				7			S		13						8		2	11^				S			32
						7			12		14						8	9	2	11*				S			33
		14				7											8*	9"	2	11^				13	12		34
						7			S		13						8	9	2	11^				S			35
		S				7			S		S						8	9	2	11							36
						7			12		14						8*	9"	2	11			13				37
		14	S			7					13						8	9		11"			3			2	38
						7^					14						13	9	8	11			4			2"	39
						7					14						13	9	8	11"			4*			2	40
		S				7					13						10^	9	8	11			4			2	41
		S				7					10			12			S		8	11			4	9*		2	42
						7					10			13			8	9"		11			4^	14		2	43
		12				7					10						14	9		11				13		2	44
	13	9	8			7				14							12			11					4	2	45
		9	10			7			13	14							8			11					12	2	46
7	25	16	18	7	3	42	11	-	11	2	19	-	1	1	-	2	20	26	21	26	-	1	12	1	1	9	A
4	1	11	3	3	1	-	2	-	12	5	14	-	5	3	1	1	9	2	1	4	1	1	1	6	2	-	S
2	1	2	2	1	1	3	3	-	1	4	7	-	-	1	-	-	1	15	2	8	-	-	2	1	-	1	G

	Bracewell	Lehmann	Collins	Salako	Neilson	Hayward	Beardsley	Brown	Uhlenbbek	Moody	Peschisolido	Arendse	Davis	Cornwall	Brooker	Scott	Smith (N)	Horsfield	Finnan	Hayles	Keller	Brazier	Albert	Betsy	McAnespie	Smith (J)	
		9	7	11		4			2		10	S	8				S	16									1
	8"	S		15		14			2		10#	S					7*	9				12					R
	8"			16		7			2		10	S					14	9		11!		3					2
	8"	16	14		4	7			S			S					10	9#	2	11!							3
	8*	16		S	2	7			12		10"						14	9!	4	11		3					R
	8		2	S		7					10	S					12	9	11	S							4
		9!	7#	8"		10			15			S					4		2	11	S		16				5

	Bracewell	Lehmann	Collins	Salako	Neilson	Hayward	Beardsley	Brown	Uhlenbbek	Moody	Peschisolido	Arendse	Davis	Cornwall	Brooker	Scott	Smith (N)	Horsfield	Finnan	Hayles	Keller	Brazier	Albert	Betsy	McAnespie	Smith (J)	
	8	9	4*	11	S	15	7	S								S											1/1
	8	9!		11	S	10	7#		2	16	15	S													S		1/2
	8	9	2		S	10	7		S					16	11!												2/1
	8	9	2"		12	10	7		11*			S			S	S											2/2
		9#	7		S	11	16		2		10!	S	8"				14							15			3

Barry Hayles: Fulham had to break the club transfer record and pay Bristol Rovers £2 million for Hayles in November 1998. A late entrant into the professional ranks, striker Hayles struggled in his early months at Fulham and eight goals in 30 appearances was a modest return on the investment. But once he settled his pace, control and strength made him a regular scorer at a higher level. Serious injury in 2002 undermined his time at the Cottage and in 2004 he moved on to Sheffield United.

Neil Smith: Although Smith was signed by Adams from Gillingham in the 1997 close season, he proved his worth in midfield under Keegan and kept his place in the squad for two seasons. In all, he played in 87 games for Fulham before he was transferred to Reading in 1999.

Paul Trollope: A natural left-footer, Trollope joined Fulham from Derby in November 1997 but struggled to hold down a regular first team place. He was a useful squad player but 30 of his 98 appearances for Fulham were as a substitute. He was a full Welsh international who moved to Coventry in 2002 and later managed Bristol Rovers.

Wayne Collins: Before signing for Fulham in January 1998, Collins had played for Crewe and Sheffield Wednesday. A hard working and competitive right sided player, Collins played 21 times in the Championship season and 79 times altogether for Fulham before rejoining Crewe in 2001.

8.

Fulham's French Revolution: 2000-01

Background

After winning the Second Division title in such style, Keegan had set the bar very high and succeeding him was going to be a huge challenge. Selecting Paul Bracewell was very much the safety first option but it proved to be the dustcart after the Lord Mayor's Parade. Bracewell had had an illustrious playing career, but one blighted by injury. With Stoke, Everton, Sunderland and Newcastle, he had been a successful midfield player, winning League, FA Cup and England honours. He was one of Keegan's first signings in the autumn of 1997 and combined playing with a coaching role. When his mentor departed for the England job, it seemed appointing Bracewell would ensure continuity.

But there was a very big difference. Although a good player, a respected coach and a shrewd tactician, Bracewell suffered one huge shortcoming that was even more obvious after Keegan: he was boring, very, very boring. Where Keegan would put on more strikers when things were not going Fulham's way, it seemed the ultra-cautious Bracewell's preferred line up was a flat back eight and two sweepers. In a six-game run in December 1999, Fulham lost just once, but scored only one goal, and that was an own goal. The chairman had not invested millions to watch four successive goalless draws.

With the Cottagers destined for a respectable but uninspiring mid-table position in their first season back in the second tier, Bracewell paid the price for being dull as well as unsuccessful. He was sacked with just six games of 1999-2000 to go. Karl-Heinz Reidle, aided and abetted by his former Liverpool manager, Roy Evans, saw Fulham through to the end of that season in a caretaker capacity before a new man was appointed as the long-term successor. And he was a very risky but ultimately inspired choice that nobody had anticipated.

When the French national side delighted viewers in the 1982 World Cup and 1984 European Championship, most of the limelight was taken by Michel Platini. But alongside him in midfield was the equally gifted Jean Tigana. He had won 52 French caps and a host of club honours with Bordeaux and Marseilles before turning to coaching. If he registered on the radar of anyone in the UK as a coach it was when his Monaco side knocked Manchester United out of the Champions League in 1996-97. Hugely respected in Europe, Tigana was an unknown quantity in England and knew little of English League football, but he was the man the Fulham board chose, the club's first non-British manager.

There were echoes of a similar decision an earlier Fulham board made in 1934. That summer, they invited a former player, Jimmy Hogan, to succeed the sacked James McIntyre. Hogan had been no more than an average player at the Cottage in the Edwardian era but had subsequently become a widely acclaimed coach in Europe, helping the development of the game in Holland, Germany and especially Austria and Hungary. He was a genuine coach, concerned with individual skills, team tactics, training routines and diets at least one generation before his British counterparts caught on. An original thinker, he was too advanced for the Fulham players who reacted negatively to his methods. Shamefully, the board sacked him after a few months while he was recovering in hospital from appendicitis.

Although neither English nor a former player, Tigana, like Hogan, did bring original thinking to Craven Cottage. To describe his methods as revolutionary would not be an understatement but, this time, the club was ready for them. And the choice paid off with interest. In Tigana's first season, Fulham not only won the First Division to reclaim a place in the top tier after a 33-year interval, but did so playing some of the best football ever seen at Craven Cottage. Much of the football was simply sublime as the manager's continental methods gradually became second nature to his squad. His teams did not just win matches. They out-played, out-passed and out-thought opponents with a style that won plaudits from the most seasoned and cynical observers. The 2000-01 First Division Championship win was a vintage season. And Tigana did it without a huge investment in new players. Most of the regulars that season were already at the club when the Frenchman arrived. He made four key acquisitions in the close season. The first was Scotsman John Collins, a midfield player who had been with Tigana at Monaco and was the manager's ambassador on the field. He cost over £2 million, as did striker Louis Saha from Metz. Both Fabrice Fernandes and Luis Boa Morte were loan signings, from French club Rennes and Southampton respectively.

From the very first game, it was apparent that something special was happening at Craven Cottage in the autumn of 2000. Opponents were not just beaten but often swept side by some breathtaking football to which the traditional British way of playing had no effective answer. In the end, Fulham took the First Division title by 10 points from Blackburn and promotion by 14 points from Bolton in third place. Fulham won their third promotion in five seasons under the third different manager and reclaimed the place in the top tier they had surrendered 33 years earlier. Mohamed al Fayed had kept his promise and confounded the doubters.

A Perfect Start

After Fulham had won their opening game of the season 2-0 against Crewe at the Cottage, the visitors' manager Dario Gradi said, 'I would rather watch Fulham than Crewe on that performance'. And it was easy to understand why. Any doubts about Tigana's understanding of the hurly-burly of the English game, or the money spent on a striker (Saha) who had not previously performed during a loan spell at Newcastle, or the wisdom of signing the veteran Collins for a large fee, all evaporated in 90 minutes of exhilarating football. It took the Cottagers until the 64th minute to open the scoring, through substitute Hayles, but the second 10 minutes from time was a gem. Collins played a 40-yard pass that was reminiscent of Haynes to set up a chance for Saha to score the first of his 27 League goals. But it was the passing and the movement, the reluctance to waste the ball or give away possession that caught the eye. Fulham dominated from first to last and the visitors spent the afternoon chasing shadows.

Any thoughts this was a one-off were banished a week later when Fulham went to St Andrews for a televised Friday night game. Birmingham, always difficult opponents on their own ground, were swept aside to the extent that Blues manager Trevor Francis said afterwards, 'I am now beginning my fifth season as Birmingham manager and that Fulham team is the best away side I've seen play at St Andrews.' Collins started it in the first minute and Saha got a second. But it was Davis' goal just before half-time that summed up Fulham's approach. Awarded a free-kick just outside the penalty area, Davis cheekily took the kick while the Birmingham defenders were trying to sort themselves out and passed the ball to the back of the net. The Blues got a goal when it was 2-0 but never threatened Fulham's superiority.

And so it continued for another nine matches, with the Cottagers collecting 33 points from their first 11 games, by far their best start to a season. Not only was the skill higher than most First Division sides, but so was the fitness, as shown by the number of goals Fulham scored in the latter stages of games. The pressure they exerted was relentless, and lasted for the full 90 minutes as was apparent in the home game against Stockport. Although Hayles put the Cottagers ahead in the opening minutes, Stockport equalised almost immediately with what proved to be their only shot on target. It took Fulham until the 58th minute to score again, a superb Collins free-kick, and then Hayles and Boa Morte made the scoreline more convincing. The statistics highlighted Fulham's superiority. They had 11 shots on target to County's one, 15 off target to three, 10 corners to two, and conceded eight fouls compared with 18.

Winning at Norwich on Bank Holiday Monday showed that Tigana's men could also dig in and grind out a result. The only goal came three minutes from time, Boa Morte rounding off a three-man passing move. But it was a bad-tempered encounter which drew nine yellow cards (five for Norwich and four for Fulham). But another televised game, on Sunday at home to Barnsley, showed the Tigana method at its best. Dave Bassett, the Tykes manager, said, 'It was deckchairs and cigars. I don't think Tigana will be ringing me to buy any of my players.' Fulham took less than five minutes to score, Saha heading home a free-kick from Fernandes, deputising for the injured Collins. Saha, following up, got his second on the half hour when the goalkeeper could only parry a Hayles effort. And on the stroke of half-time, he completed his hat-trick when Goldbaek was brought down. Hayles made it 4-0 in the 58th minute from Goldbaek's cross and, after Appleby had the temerity to score for the visitors, Boa Morte made it 5-1 at the final whistle. Barnsley were simply overwhelmed by a Fulham side that looked different class.

And so it continued for the rest of September. Burnley were beaten 3-1 at the Cottage, which included a spectacular long-range free-kick by Goldbaek, and a week later the 3-0 win at Forest made it seven wins on the trot, beating the previous best start to season in 1958-59. This win at the City Ground was achieved without Collins and Davis but a superb Hayles lob together with a Fernandes strike and Saha penalty earned a convincing win. Gillingham at home (3-0) and Bolton away (2-0) were beaten without conceding a goal. Hayles was the chief tormentor of the Gills while at Bolton, Boa Morte opened the scoring after just 12 seconds. Both opposition managers (Andy Hessenthaler and Sam Allardyce) were full of praise for Fulham's style and thought the divisional Championship could be wrapped up by Christmas.

The visit of Blackburn at the start of October proved to be the hardest test so far and the result took on an extra significance later in the season. Rovers, who

Fernandes scores the second at Forest in September.

had made an indifferent start, went into a fourth minute lead through Jansen but Fernandes equalised 20 minutes later. It took a second half penalty by Saha, awarded after he had been tripped, to secure the 10th win but the Cottagers made it hard for themselves with careless passing in the final third. Palace were overshadowed in midweek at the Cottage in a physical encounter. After Saha opened the scoring on 10 minutes, Ruddick levelled but Clark put Fulham ahead before the break and sealed the win with his second on the hour. There were plenty of chances to add to the score but 3-1 was enough to open up a four-point lead at the top of the table and equal Newcastle's First Division record of 11 consecutive wins at the start of 1992-93. The Magpies at that time were managed by Keegan.

A Dip of Sorts

But then the winning stopped and by the time the Cottagers next collected three points, they had drawn twice, lost once and for the first and only time, surrendered top spot in the table. But this was a temporary aberration and in November, normal service was resumed. The magnificent start ended at Molineux. Wolves had taken six points from Fulham the previous season and had done their homework on how to stop the Cottagers playing, which at times inclined to the very physical. Although denied an obvious penalty and having several acceptable chances, Tigana's men could not break down a stubborn Wolves defence while the home side presented very little threat to Taylor's goal. They remained unbeaten after the 0-0 draw but lost their 100 per cent record.

The unbeaten record went days later, on a Tuesday evening at the Cottage to fifth-placed Preston, managed by David Moyes. In a game disrupted by fouls and offsides, Fulham looked lethargic and static and lost to a strange goal in the 67th minute. Appleton took a corner for Preston and curled the ball to the near post where it appeared to strike Taylor on the knee and go into the net. Collins was honest enough to admit that this sort of result had been coming for a week or two. The issue was not losing but the way the team bounced back when some in the media were claiming the Fulham bubble had burst. Watford now led the table by a single point after 13 matches.

During the excitement of the promotion chase, the Cottagers were involved in a longer-than-usual run in the Worthington (League) Cup, which for once did not prove a distraction to the League ambitions. Fulham actually lost their unbeaten record in their third game of the season, a Worthington Cup tie at Northampton's Sixfields Stadium. The club from the League basement beat a weakened Fulham side 1-0 in the first leg but goals from Davis, Fernandes and Saha (2) saw Fulham through in the second. It was a similar story in round two against Chesterfield, a 1-0 defeat in the first leg followed by another 4-0 win the second at the Cottage. The third round tie at home to Wolves was a thriller. Goalless at half-time, Fulham fell behind in the 57th minute but then strikes by Boa Morte (2) and Saha gave them a 3-1 lead before the visitors made it 3-2 in the last few minutes.

Round four offered a sterner test, Premiership Derby at home, and Fulham came through with flying colours. An absorbing game was settled in the last minute when Saha got his head to Goldbaek's free-kick to make it 3-2 to Fulham. Derby had led 1-0 before Saha and Eddie Lewis put Fulham ahead. On the stroke of half-time, Derby were back on terms with a surprise equaliser and there the scores stood until

Saha's dramatic intervention in the final minute putting Fulham into the quarter-finals for the second successive season. The prize was well worth having, a trip to Anfield. The Cottagers put up a terrific fight and lost only in extra time but the 3-0 scoreline flattered Liverpool.

Dropping two points at Hillsborough a few days later meant the Cottagers had won just two points from a possible nine in a week. But this time, they scored three goals, showed a lot of resilience and probably should have won. They went behind on 42 minutes to a Sibon header, but Saha equalised two minutes after the re-start. A brilliant individual goal by Hayles eight minutes later put the visitors ahead and when Wednesday's Quinn was sent off in 63rd minute, Fulham looked good for the points. On 70 minutes, however, Morrison headed an equaliser. It took an unlikely back heel by defender Melville to give the Cottagers what looked to be a decisive edge in the final 10 minutes. Yet depleted Wednesday came back again and in the last minute Westwood put a header out of Taylor's reach, the Owls' third headed goal of the game.

Full Steam Ahead

After this pause for breath, Fulham came back even stronger and of the remaining 10 games in 2000, they won eight and drew two. They finished the year with a resounding home win over the only team to have displaced them at the top, Watford. At the halfway stage of the season, they had lost just once, they led second-placed Bolton by 10 points and were 16 clear of Blackburn in third. Never before had a Fulham team been in such a commanding position at this stage of a season.

Perhaps it was lucky that the Cottager's next opponents were bottom-of-the-table Huddersfield, who had won just once in 15 League games. Nevertheless, it took 57 minutes for Fulham to go in front, through a Saha header from a Fernandes free-kick. Thereafter the result was never in doubt. Goldbaek and Finnan both scored in the last five minutes to make the scoreline better reflect the balance of play.

After that, Wimbledon (3-0 away) and Portsmouth (3-1 home) were both outclassed as the Cottagers scored three-in-a-game for the third and fourth consecutive games. Saha and Hayles were in sparkling form and few defences could hold them. In fact the only ways were illegal and Pompey were so physical in their approach that they had two men sent off for persistent fouling. A draw in a fiercely competitive game at wet and windy Bramall Lane on a Tuesday evening was only a brief interruption to the winning sequence. All the scoring was done in the first 10 minutes, a sensational run and strike by Finnan after four minutes and a Sheffield equaliser four minutes later by D'Jaffo following a goalmouth scramble. Fulham had the better of the second half and United picked up six yellow cards keeping them out.

Fulham dominated lowly Grimsby but had to be content with a 2-1 win. The Mariners' goalkeeper Coyne was in outstanding form, and he needed to be as shots peppered his goal. In a match played at the Cottage in a strong wind and slanting rain, the supporters had to wait until the 60th minute for Saha and Clark to combine to set up Boa Morte for the opener. Saha made it 2-0 with 10 minutes remaining, a 25-yard strike, and late goal from Grimsby's Donovan came too late to affect the result. Although Fulham only got a draw the following week at Preston, they had more shots on target than Preston (7-1), more corners (5-3) and conceded fewer fouls (10-23). A Jackson header gave home side a fourth minute lead but this was their only effort on goal. Davis equalised on the hour with a 30-yard drive from a Goldbaek knockdown. North End manager Moyes said afterwards, 'In all my time as manager here, that has been the hardest game, apart from Arsenal and Everton. I thought Fulham were fantastic.'

There were three wins before Christmas, away at West Brom (3-1), at home to Tranmere (3-1) and away at Crewe (2-1). A new name appeared on the scoresheet at the Hawthorns, Latvian international Andrejs Stolcers signed for £2 million who made his debut as substitute. But it was the old guard of Boa Morte (three goals), Davis (two goals), Clark and Hayles (one each) who did the damage. These wins set up the eagerly anticipated Boxing Day fixture at home to Watford. The Hornets, managed again by Graham Taylor, were for a long period the Cottagers nearest challengers at the top of the table, and the rivalry was intensified by some of their manager's less-than-gracious comments about Fulham. The largest crowd of the season (19,373) saw a rampant Fulham destroy Watford. Hayles led the charge with a hat-trick with Saha from the penalty spot and Stolcers making it a resounding 5-0. Even though Watford had been well and truly humbled, Taylor rather churlishly said afterwards of Fulham, 'I think they have three Premiership players'. Not for the first time, his judgement was found wanting.

No Winter Break

Although the New Year started with two defeats, surprisingly in the League at Stockport and unsurprisingly in the FA Cup against Manchester United, Fulham's progress to the divisional title and a place back in the top fight was unrelenting. There were five wins and two draws in the 10 League games in January and February. At the end of February, with 12 games to go, Fulham led Bolton by 12 points and Blackburn by 16. Tigana's team was like a steamroller that kept moving forward whatever the obstacles in its path. And if it occasionally faltered, there was the consolation of knowing that their nearest rivals were slipping even more.

At Edgeley Park on New Year's Day, Fulham lost their unbeaten away record and suffered only their second defeat of the season. In an even game, Stockport took their two chances, minutes either side of half-time, while for once the Fulham attack fired blanks. Just days later, the Fulham captain Chris Coleman was involved in a serious road accident that ended his playing career. It was a dreadful blow to the 30-year-old Welshman, who had proved such an effective leader and was on the verge of leading the club to a second promotion in three seasons. Fortunately, while he never played again, the story of Coleman and Fulham had quite a bit further to run. Losing the defensive lynchpin could also have destabilised the back four but fortunately, Symons was in the wings and could step in and fill the gap alongside Melville.

Even with a much depleted side, Hayles, Clark, and Fernandes as well as Coleman were all missing, Fulham overcame Norwich at the Cottage. A goal from Saha in the first half and Boa Morte in the second got the Cottagers back on the winning track in a hard-earned victory. It was more straightforward in the return against Watford the following week, thanks to three excellent goals, two for Boa Morte and one for Saha, all the result of superbly timed runs on to accurate passes. Future Fulham player Helguson got a late consolation for the Hornets which was given despite the fact he clearly punched the ball into the net.

When Birmingham visited the Cottage, winning a point seemed to be the limit of their ambitions, even though the Cottagers were without Hayles, Saha, Boa Morte and Collins. The makeshift front line of Peter Moller, making his debut, and Stolcers never really got going and a goal by Grainger from a controversial free-kick gave the Blues a surprise win. For the midweek trip to nearby Loftus Road, Fulham welcomed back Saha and German international Reidle returned as substitute after a long lay-off with injury. He scored the second and decisive goal from a close range header in the 70th minute. Moller was gifted the first on the stroke of half-time, his soft shot squirming through the goalkeeper's hands.

There were two draws against two Yorkshire clubs in quick succession, 1-1 at home to Sheffield United and 0-0 away at Barnsley, two games in which the Cottagers had the better of the play but were unable to break down resolute defences. Both the Blades and the Tykes were happier with the point than Fulham. Forest also proved to be difficult opponents to break down at the Cottage. In seventh place and with an eye on the Play-offs, the visitors took the game to the Cottagers but fell behind to a well-worked goal in the 19th minute, Saha volleying in Boa Morte's pull back from the left. Forest pressed very hard and gave the Fulham defence a difficult afternoon but could not find an equaliser.

Turf Moor on a Tuesday night in February is not a very welcoming place and

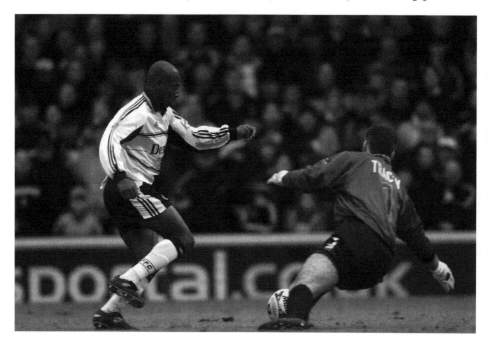

Boa Morte rounds the Sheffield United 'keeper to score in February.

so it proved as Tigana's team slipped to a 2-1 defeat, despite taking the lead with a Hayles header. The Clarets winning goal came two minutes from time after an even game. Fulham had not won at Gillingham since 1988, and had lost on their last four visits to the Priestfield, and so the 2-0 win days after the Burnley defeat was especially welcome. Both goals came in the last 15 minutes and substitute Boa Morte was Fulham's match winner, setting up the first goal for Collins and scoring the second himself.

Although they trailed Fulham by 12 points, Bolton were in second place when they visited the Cottage for a Sunday lunchtime kick-off. Despite hitting the wood-work several times and seeing a number of shots cleared off the line, Fulham could not add to Hayles 40th minute goal. Their cause was not helped by Boa Morte's dismissal in the 77th minute for retaliation after a bad tackle by Elliott. In between Hayles' goal and the red card, Frandsen scored for Bolton from a free-kick and so after 90 minutes, the gap remained at 12 points. A second home game in six days produced another three points after a comfortable 2-0 win over QPR. A Saha penalty after Finnan had been fouled had given the Cottagers the lead 37 minutes into the game and they had to wait until Clark's last-minute goal to make the scoreline more decisive.

Then came two away games in six days, six goals for, one against and six more points. At Selhurst Park, two Boa Morte goals, one in each half, took care of a hard-working but predictable Palace side, while at Prenton Park, Tranmere were thrashed 4-1 in a televised match. To their credit, Rovers tried to play football against Fulham but once Saha opened the scoring after three minutes the writing was on the wall. Further goals from Hayles, Clark and Saha emphasised the Cottagers' superiority and Rovers only reply was a last minute goal by Osborn.

Behind the scenes there was some activity. Tigana spent £4 million on another Frenchman, Newcastle's Alain Goma, a central-defender who was to replace Coleman. Goma was to prove an excellent signing, but in the Premiership in subsequent seasons rather than Division One as he made just two appearances in the promotion run-in. The manager also let Fernandes go under something of a cloud to Glasgow Rangers. The player was exciting and unpredictable but his attitude did not endear him to the Tigana. There was also an England Under 21 call up for Sean Davis who looked to be on his way to becoming the first Fulham player to play for England since George Cohen in the 1960s.

A Lap of Honour

The Cottagers went into the final full month of the season 17 points clear of the team in second place and 19 ahead of third, and there were just eight games to go. It was just a question of when not if Fulham clinched promotion and the title. They inched their way towards the finishing line with a hard-fought 0-0 draw at home to West Brom. The visitors worked for their point, hustling Fulham out of their normal rhythm and although they posed few threats to the Fulham goal, were probably worth their point.

Blackburn had become one of the few threats to Fulham's procession to the title and a midweek visit to Ewood Park for a televised meeting was in effect a title decider. Rovers manager Graeme Souness stirred the pot beforehand by claiming his team on current form were the best in the division. And so it seemed after six minutes when Jansen gave the home side the lead and then, after Brevett was sent off after a tangle with Flitcroft, the odds swung heavily in favour of Rovers. Tigana took off an attacker (Hayles) and brought on defender Neilson and, two minutes after the red card, the scores were level. Goalkeeper Friedel and full-back Berg collided going for Finnan's high ball into the area and Saha was on hand to pick up the pieces. In the second half, 10-man Fulham withstood all the threat Rovers could offer until in added time the unthinkable happened. Goldbaek played a ball forward to Clark whose shot was deflected off Berg into the path of Davis. The Fulham midfield man kept his head and placed the ball past Friedel into the net for a famous victory. Even the normally impassive Tigana danced a jig down the touchline because he now accepted promotion was a certainty. 'Focus and discipline' said the manager afterwards, explaining his side's victory.

Winning at Huddersfield three days later confirmed promotion mathematically with five games to spare. It was a dour game. After a goalless first half, Fulham went ahead with a Saha penalty on 66 minutes, awarded for a foul on Boa Morte. The Terriers managed to get back on terms 12 minutes later when Facey raced through to beat Melville and Taylor to score. But six minutes later came the clincher, the goal which ensured promotion and earned a club record 14th away win. Finnan fed Boa Morte and when the 'keeper inexplicably rushed out of his goal to the angle of the box, he slipped the ball past him into the empty net.

Davis has just scored the dramatic last minute winner in the vital game at Blackburn in April.

Saha from the spot in the promotion-clincher at Huddersfield.

Davis equalises against Sheffield Wednesday at the Cottage in April.

In the remaining five games, there was a feeling that the players were going through the motions. They won one and drew three and four of the five goals they scored were from penalties. A 1-1 home draw with Sheffield Wednesday was followed by a 1-1 away draw at Portsmouth, a game which marked Goma's debut. Sadly this lasted less than half the game as he was injured in a collision with Pompey's Bradbury. Both goals in the 2-0 home win over Wolves came from the spot, converted by Saha, a game best remembered now as the last of Simon Morgan's 418

Justifiable celebrations after the final home game.

The architects of the success - chairman Fayed and manager Tigana

Fulham appearances. He came on as substitute for his only appearance of a season in which he had been struggling with injury. Having played so many games in the lower divisions for the Cottagers, it was appropriate that Morgan's finale should be in Division One.

Fulham signed off at home with a desultory 1-1 draw against Wimbledon, Boa Morte getting the goal from the spot. But the mood was celebratory and after the final whistle, the Division One trophy was presented to the joint captains, Coleman and Melville, in a spectacular ceremony choreographed at Harrods. All the players, management team and the chairman were on the pitch to receive the well-deserved accolades from supporters. Although the final game was a damp squib, a 1-0 defeat at Grimsby, nothing could dim the brilliance of the performance over the previous nine months or take away from the fact that this was Fulham's best-ever season. The fact it lacked a dramatic finale was a measure of the team's superiority throughout the campaign.

Reflections

This was a season that would live long in the memory of Fulham supporters and was at least the equal of anything seen in the halcyon days of Haynes, Leggat, Cohen and Mullery in the 1960s. Unlike that earlier period, 2000-01 was a genuine team triumph rather than a success built on a handful of outstanding individuals. And a measure of the team's triumph was the number of club records that were established in the campaign, which suggested that it achieved more than the two previous promotion teams and at a higher level.

Most away wins (14) beating by two the total under Micky Adams and Kevin Keegan.
Most away points (48), five more than in 1996-97.
Fewest defeats (5), two fewer than in 1998-99.
Fewest away defeats (3), one less than in 1996-97.
Most home and away 'doubles' (10), one more than in 1998-99.
The points total of 101 equalled the previous best of two seasons earlier.
The defensive record of just 32 conceded equalled the goals against in 1922-23 and 1998-99.
Fewest away goals conceded (18) was the same in as in 1996-97.

In 2000-01 Tigana's team set the standard throughout the country. Fulham became the first side to break the 100-point twice while the wonderful 11-match winning start equalled the previous best in Division One. In addition, the Cottagers had the best defensive record in the Nationwide League, the largest number of victories, the fewest defeats, the best goal difference, the highest number of points and were the highest scorers in all four divisions.

Not surprisingly, Tigana won the League Managers' Association Manager of the Year award, while Collins and Clark won Player of the Month awards during the season. Saha was the Nationwide Player of the Year for 2000, the Four-Four-Two Division One Player of the Season, and, as the highest scorer in all four divisions, the winner of the Four-Four-Two Golden Boot Award. The International honours also came in the direction of several Fulham players, for Boa Morte (Portugal), Coleman (Wales), Finnan (Eire), Goldbaek (Denmark), Hayles (Jamaica), Lewis (USA), Melville (Wales), Peschisolido (Canada), Phelan (Eire), Stolcers (Latvia), Symons (Wales) and Taylor (Northern Ireland). In addition, Under-21 caps were won by Davis for England and McAnespie for Scotland.

A measure of the regard in which the Fulham players were held by their Division One peers is that six of them, goalkeeper Taylor, defenders Finnan and Coleman, midfield players Clark and Davis, and striker Saha, were voted into the PFA Division One Team Of 2000-01.

This was no ordinary promotion win and the season remains a landmark in Fulham's 123-year history. But, having achieved their objective of getting back into the big time, the bigger issue of staying there confronted them once the celebrations had died down. The response to the challenge of Premier League football probably exceeded the expectations of the Fulham faithful. Going into 2012-13, Fulham were starting their 12th consecutive Premier season and only seven clubs (Manchester United, Arsenal, Chelsea, Liverpool, Tottenham Hotspur, Everton and Aston Villa) had been in the top flight continuously for longer. Attendances are at near-full capacity most weeks, the ground is to be redeveloped, a European Final has been reached and the youth scheme is now producing some promising talent. That unforgettable success under Tigana in 2000-01 was the start not the end of a story that hopefully has some way still to run. The corner shop of the early 1990s had been transformed into the superstore of the modern era.

Summary Statistics

End	Played	Points	Position
September	9	27	1
October	14	35	2
November	19	48	1
December	24	61	1
January	29	70	1
February	34	78	1
March	38	88	1
April	45	101	1
Final	**46**	**101**	**1**

	H	A	Total
P	23	23	**46**
W	16	14	**30**
D	5	6	**11**
L	2	3	**5**
F	49	41	**90**
A	14	18	**32**
Pts	53	48	**101**

0 points v	*1 point v*	*2 points v*	*3 points v*	*4 points v*	*6 points v*
	Preston NE	Sheffield U	Birm C	Barnsley	Blackburn R
		Sheffield W	Burnley	Bolton W	Crewe A
			Grimsby T	Portsmouth	Crystal P
			Stockport C	West Brom A	Gillingham
				Wimbledon	Huddersfield T
				Wolves	Norwich C
					Notts F
					Queen's Park R
					Tranmere R
					Watford
0 points	**1 point**	**4 points**	**12 points**	**24 points**	**60 points**

The Championship Squad: 2000-01

Maik Taylor: After an ever-present in Keegan's Championship season, goalkeeper Taylor missed just two games under Tigana and was beaten just 30 times in 44 games. Despite this, Fulham paid a huge fee for Edwin Van der Sar before the start of their first Premier season. Taylor remained loyally on the bench for three seasons but after 228 games in six seasons left the Cottage for Birmingham in 2003.

Steve Finnan: Signed by Keegan for a modest fee in the early months of 1998-99, Finnan matured into a top class defender, stylish and unhurried. He missed just one game in the Tigana Championship season and became a regular in the Republic of Ireland side. He went on to play for Fulham for two seasons in the top flight before switching to Liverpool in 2003.

Rufus Brevett: Another who won two Championship medals in three seasons, Brevett played in 39 of the 46 games at left-back and, despite the sceptics claiming he was not a naturally talented defender, he held his own in the top flight over the next two seasons until he was transferred to West Ham in 2003.

Andy Melville: A relative newcomer, the Welsh central-defender was signed by Bracewell, a former Sunderland teammate, on a free transfer in 1999. Melville had spent three years with Oxford before a five-year stint with the Black Cats. He replaced Symons at the heart of the defence and took over as captain the closing months of the season after Coleman's car crash. After 181 games, Melville moved on to West Ham in 2004.

Chris Coleman: Sadly for the Fulham captain, this memorable season was his last as player after 162 games for the Cottagers. Having played in all 25 games up to the turn of the year, Coleman was seriously injured in a road accident that threatened more than the end of his playing career. He remained at major presence at the club, however, eventually succeeding Tigana as manager in 2003. He is now manager of the Welsh national side.

Bjarne Goldbaek: The Danish international and right sided midfield player was signed by Bracewell from Chelsea in 2000 for a sizeable fee and featured regularly in Tigana's Championship side, missing just two games. With the arrival of some expensive signings in the 2001 close season, he became a squad player in the top flight and left the Cottage for a German club in 2003.

Lee Clark: In his early months as manager, Bracewell went back to his old club and paid Sunderland £3 million for midfield player Clark, a Fulham record. A Geordie, Clark had also spent seven years at Newcastle and he had helped both north east clubs to win promotion to the top flight. At the Cottage, he provided guile and craft in midfield, although he lacked a little pace. He missed only one game in 2000-01 and made 178 appearances in six seasons, two of which were lost to injury. After playing, Clark went into management, first with Huddersfield and currently with Birmingham.

Louis Saha: The French striker was a sensation when Tigana bought him from Metz in June 2000 for £2.1 million. With his total of 32 goals in his first season he was the highest scorer in any division in England. His lightning pace, great control and predatory instincts made him the first Fulham player to score 30 goals in a season since Jezzard in 1953-54. Not surprisingly, he found it tougher in the top flight, and injuries started to accumulate. When he was back to his best again in 2003-04, Manchester United paid almost £13 million for him, a Fulham record.

John Collins: Although nearing the veteran stage, Tigana paid Everton £2 million for the 32-year-old Scottish international midfielder. He had previously signed him for Monaco from Celtic and the two had enjoyed a successful partnership. At the Cottage, he was wonderfully creative in midfield; his vision and distribution were a pivotal part of the team's style until injuries led to his retirement in 2003. His managerial career has taken in Hibernian, Charleroi (Belgium) and Livingston, where is currently director of operations.

Luis Boa Morte: Initially signed on loan from Southampton by Tigana, the move was made permanent after 12 months for £1.6 million. Starting with Sporting Lisbon, Boa Morte signed for Arsenal before moving to the Dell in 1999. He had much more success at Fulham, scoring 18 goals in 39 appearances in his first season and 52 in his 238 games for Fulham, mostly playing down the left side. An unpredictable and at times volatile player, Portuguese international Boa Morte, a match winner on his day, moved on to West Ham in 2007 for a large fee.

2000-01

League Division One Manager : Jean Tigana

No		Date	V	Opponents	R	H-T	F-T	Scorers	Attend	Taylor	Finnan	Brevett	Melville	Coleman	Lewis	Goldbaek	Clark	Saha
1	A	12	H	Crewe A	W	0-0	2-0	Hayles, Saha	11,157	1	2	3	4	5	6	7	8^	9*
2		18	A	Birmingham C	W	3-1	3-1	Collins, Saha, Davis	21,659	1	2	3	4	5		7	8	9*
3		26	H	Stockport C	W	1-1	4-1	Hayles 2, Collins, Boa Morte	11,009	1	2	3	4	5		7*	8	9^
4		28	A	Norwich C	W	0-0	1-0	Boa Morte	16,678	1	2	3	4	5	12	7*	8	9
5	S	10	H	Barnsley	W	3-0	5-1	Saha 3, Hayles, Boa Morte	10,437	1	2	3	4	5	12	7*	8	9
6		12	H	Burnley	W	0-1	3-1	Goldbaek, Saha 2	11,863	1	2	3	4	5	12	7	8	9*
7		16	A	Nottingham F	W	0-0	3-0	Saha, Fernandes, Hayles	18,737	1	2	3^	4	5		7	8	9*
8		23	H	Gillingham	W	1-0	3-0	Hayles 2, Clark	13,032	1	2		4	5		7	8	9*
9		30	A	Bolton W	W	1-0	2-0	Boa Morte 2	19,924	1	2		4	5		7	8	
10	O	15	H	Blackburn R	W	1-1	2-1	Fernandes, Saha	15,247	1	2		4	5	12	7*	8	13
11		18	H	Crystal Palace	W	2-1	3-1	Saha, Clark 2	16,040	1	2			5	12	7*	8	9
12		21	A	Wolverhampton W	D	0-0	0-0		21,080	1	2	3	4	5		7	8	9*
13		24	H	Preston NE	L	0-0	0-1		14,354	1	2	3	4	5		7*	8	9
14		28	A	Sheffield W	D	0-1	3-3	Saha, Hayles, Melville	17,559	1	2	3'	4	5		12	8	9
15	N	4	H	Huddersfield T	W	0-0	3-0	Saha, Goldbaek, Finnan	13,108	1	2	3		5		7	8	9^
16		11	A	Wimbledon	W	1-0	3-0	Saha 2, Hayles	14,071	1	2	3	4	5		7*	8	9'
17		18	H	Portsmouth	W	1-1	3-1	Hayles 2, Clark	19,005	1	2	3	4	5		7*	8	9
18		21	A	Sheffield U	D	1-1	1-1	Finnan	16,041	1	2	3	4	5		7^	8'	9*
19		25	H	Grimsby T	W	0-0	2-1	Boa Morte, Saha	12,107	1	2	3		5		7*	8	12
20	D	2	A	Preston NE	D	0-1	1-1	Davis	16,047	1	2	3	4	5		7	8	9
21		9	A	West Bromwich A	W	2-0	3-1	Davis 2, Stolcers	23,301	1	2	3	4	5		7*	8	9^
22		16	H	Tranmere R	W	2-1	3-1	Clark, Boa Morte 2	13,157	1	2	3	4	5		12	8	9^
23		23	A	Crewe A	W	0-1	2-1	Boa Morte, Hayles	6,925	1	2	3	4	5		7	8	12
24		26	H	Watford	W	2-0	5-0	Saha, Hayles 3, Stolcers	19,373	1	2	3	4	5^		7	8	9*
25	J	1	A	Stockport C	L	0-1	0-2		6,100	1	2	3	4	5		7	8	9
26		13	H	Norwich C	W	1-0	2-0	Saha, Boa Morte	16,062	1	2	3	4			7		9
27		20	A	Watford	W	0-0	3-1	Boa Morte 2, Saha	18,333	1	2	3	4			7		9
28		27	H	Birmingham C	L	0-0	0-1		17,077	1	2	3	4		12	7	8	
29		31	A	Queen's Park R	W	1-0	2-0	Moller. Riedle	16,403	1	2	3	4			7		9
30	F	4	H	Sheffield U	D	1-1	1-1	Boa Morte	12,480	1	2	3	4			7*	8	9
31		10	A	Barnsley	D	0-0	0-0		14,654	1	2		4			7	8	9
32		17	H	Nottingham F	W	1-0	1-0	Saha	17,425	1	2	3	4			7	8	9
33		20	A	Burnley	L	0-0	1-2	Hayles	15,737	1	2	3	4			7	8	
34		24	A	Gillingham	W	0-0	2-0	Collins, Boa Morte	9,931	1	2	3	4			7	8	9
35	M	4	H	Bolton W	D	1-0	1-1	Hayles	16,468	1	2	3	4			7	8	9
36		10	H	Queen's Park R	W	1-0	2-0	Saha, Clark	16,021	1	2	3	4			7	8	9
37		17	A	Crystal Palace	W	1-0	2-0	Boa Morte 2	21,133	1	2	3	4			7	8	12
38		30	A	Tranmere R	W	2-0	4-1	Saha 2, Hayles, Clark	12,362	1	2	3	4				8	9
39	A	7	H	West Bromwich A	D	0-0	0-0		17,795	1	2	3	4			12	8	9
40		11	A	Blackburn R	W	1-1	2-1	Saha, Davis	21,578	1	2	3	4			7	8	9
41		14	A	Huddersfield T	W	0-0	2-1	Saha, Boa Morte	15,882	1	2	3	4			7	8	9
42		16	H	Sheffield W	D	0-1	1-1	Davis	17,500		2	3	4			7	8	9
43		21	A	Portsmouth	D	0-1	1-1	Saha	17,651	1	2	3	4			7	8	9
44		24	H	Wolverhampton W	W	1-0	2-0	Saha 2	15,375	1		3	4				8	9
45		28	H	Wimbledon	D	0-0	1-1	Boa Morte	18,576	1	2		12			7	8	9
46	M	8	A	Grimsby T	L	0-1	0-1		8,706		2		4			7	8	9

								Apps		44	45	39	42	25	1	41	45	39
								Sub		-	-	-	1	-	6	3	-	4
								Goals		-	2	-	1	-	-	2	7	27

Collins J	Boa Morte	Fernandes	Betsy	Hayles	Davis	Hayward	Collins W	Trollope	Symons	Willock	Sahnoun	Stolcers	Phelan	Moller	Riedle	Neilson	Hahnemann	Goma	Morgan	Peschisolido	Cornwall	Knight	McAnespie	Hudson	Hammond	#
10	11'	12	13	14																						1
10	12			11	6																					2
10	12	13		11	6																					3
10	13	14		11^	6																					4
	13	10		11^	6	14																				5
	13	10		11^	6'		14																			6
	12	10		11			6	13																		7
10	12	6		11			3																			8
10	11	6		9					3																	9
10	11^	6		9					3																	10
10	11^	6		13	14				3	4																11
10	12	6		11																						12
12	13	6^		10	11'				14																	13
10	13	6*		11^	7				14																	14
10		12		11	6*				4	13																15
10	11^	12		13	6				14																	16
	12	6		10	11^						13															17
	12	6		10	11			13			14															18
	9	6		10	11				4																	19
	10*	6		12	11																					20
12	13	6'		10	11							14														21
	11	6*		13	14						10'	7														22
	11			10	10^		13					6														23
	12	6'		10*	11				13			14														24
	12	6^			11'						13	14														25
	11		8*		10				5		12	6^	13													26
	10	6			11				5																	27
		6			11				5			10^		9	13											28
		6			11				5					10*	12											29
	10	6			11				5						12											30
	10	6			11			3	5						12											31
10	11				6				5			12		13	14											32
10	11	12		9	6				5						13											33
10	12			11	6				5						13	14										34
10	12			11	6				5																	35
10	12			11	6				5			14			13											36
10	11			9	6				5								13									37
10				11	6				5					7												38
10				11	6				5					7	13											39
10				11	6				5								12									40
	11				12				5		10	6		14	13											41
10	11			12	6				5			14			13			1								42
10	11		12		6				13						14				5							43
10		11			6		2		5		12			13	7					14						44
10	11				6		3		5			14			13				4							45
	11		13	12	6							10	3					1	5							46
25	21	23	2	28	37	-	3	22	22	-	2	8	1	2	1	-	2	3	-							A
2	18	6	3	7	3	1	2	2	2	1	5	7	1	3	13	3	-	-	1							S
3	18	2	-	18	6	-	-	-	-	-	-	2	-	1	1	-	-	-	-							G

				FA CUP							1	2	3	4			7	8	9
3	J	7	H	Manchester U	L	1-1	1-2	Fernandes	19,178							6			
				WORTHINGTON CUP															
1/1	A	22	A	Northampton T	L	0-1	0-1		3,487										
2/1	S	5	H	Northampton T	W	1-1	4-1	Davis, Fernandes, Saha 2	5,302				3			6*		8	12
2/1		19	A	Chesterfield	L	0-0	0-1		3,710		1						8		
2/2		27	H	Chesterfield	W	1-0	4-0	Hayward, Symons, Hayles, Boa Morte	4,800		1					6		8	
3	N	1	H	Wolverhampton W	W	0-0	3-2	Boa Morte 2, Saha	6,763		1	12		4			7'	2	8	9
4		28	H	Derby C	W	2-2	3-2	Saha 2, Lewis	11,761		1			4		11	7		9
5	D	13	A	Liverpool	L	0-0	0-3	(aet)	20,144		1	2	3	4	5		7	8	9

	1	2	3	4			7	8	9
Apps	6	2	3	4	1	6	4	5	4
Sub	-	1	-	-	-	-	-	-	1
Goals	-	-	-	-	-	1	-	-	5

Fabrice Fernandes: Another Frenchman who arrived with Tigana, Fernandes was signed on loan from Rennes. He was an exciting, individual talent, who was most effective on the flanks. At times too elaborate, he also had an uneasy relationship with authority. The Championship year, when he played in 29 of the games, was his only season at the Cottage after which he played for Rangers, Southampton, Bolton and Doncaster without ever fulfilling his obvious potential.

Barry Hayles: Keegan's big-money signing of 1998 blossomed under Tigana and in 2000-01 enjoyed his best Fulham season with 18 goals. With Saha and Boa Morte, Hayles shared a remarkable 63 goals, and these three scored more than 18 clubs in the division could manage. Although London-born, he was capped by Jamaica.

11*	6							5		10	12											3
11	7	8*		12	9	4		5			3		2	1		10^	13					1/1
11	4		9^	7	13	2							5	1			10					1/2
11				7				5					2			9	10*	6	3	4	12	2/1
9	14	10^	13		11'		3	5					4				7*	12	2			2/2
11	13			10		6	3*	5														3
	6		10			2	3	5	8													4
	6*		10	11					12													5

·	6	5	2	3	3	3	4	3	6	·	2	·	1	·	4	2	·	·	2	1	3	1	2	·	A
·	·	2	·	1	1	1	·	·	·	·	·	2	·	·	·	·	·	·	·	1	·	1	·	1	S
·	1	2	·	1	1	1	·	·	1	·	·	·	·	·	·	·	·	·	·	·	·	·	·	·.	G

Sean Davis: The first player to emerge from Fulham's juniors since the 1980s, Davis became the only player to play for Fulham in the four divisions of the League. He made a substitute appearance in Division Three for the Micky Adams promotion team, made his full debut and five other substitute appearances in the Keegan Second Division side and missed only six games when Tigana's team won the First Division title. A very competitive and skilful midfield player, Davis then had three Premier seasons at the Cottage which took him into the full England squad. He moved to Spurs in 2004 and later played for Portsmouth and Bolton.

Kit Symons: The arrival of Melville meant Symons unluckily lost the central-defensive role alongside Coleman. But in this Championship season, he still managed 24 appearances and was able to step in when Coleman was seriously injured. He did not get much of a look in once Fulham were in the top flight and in 2001 he finished his playing career at Crystal Palace. Symons in now back at Fulham in a managerial role and involved with Coleman again with Welsh national team.